LINCOLN CHRISTIAN COLLEGE AND SEMINARY

P9-DDW-235

# Captivating
## Children's Sermons

# Captivating
## Children's Sermons

Crafting Powerful, Practical Messages

Beth Edington Hewitt

**BakerBooks**
Grand Rapids, Michigan

© 2005 by Beth Edington Hewitt

Published by Baker Books
a division of Baker Publishing Group
P.O. Box 6287, Grand Rapids, MI 49516-6287
www.bakerbooks.com

Printed in the United States of America

All rights reserved. No part of this publication may be reproduced, stored in a retrieval system, or transmitted in any form or by any means—for example, electronic, photocopy, recording—without the prior written permission of the publisher. The only exception is brief quotations in printed reviews.

Library of Congress Cataloging-in-Publication Data
Hewitt, Beth Edington.
    Captivating children's sermons : crafting powerful, practical
messages / Beth Edington Hewitt.
        p.    cm.
    Includes bibliographical references.
    ISBN 0-8010-6544-5 (pbk.)
    1. Preaching to children. I. Title.
BV4235.C4H49  2005
252'.53—dc22                                              2005012322

Unless otherwise noted, Scripture is taken from the HOLY BIBLE, NEW INTERNATIONAL VERSION®. NIV®. Copyright © 1973, 1978, 1984 by International Bible Society. Used by permission of Zondervan. All rights reserved.

Scripture marked NLT is taken from the *Holy Bible*, New Living Translation, copyright © 1996. Used by permission of Tyndale House Publishers, Inc., Wheaton, Illinois 60189. All rights reserved.

Scripture marked RSV is taken from the Revised Standard Version of the Bible, copyright 1952 [2nd edition, 1971] by the Division of Christian Education of the National Council of the Churches of Christ in the United States of America. Used by permission. All rights reserved.

Published in association with the literary agency of Wolgemuth & Associates.

To my parents,
for teaching me to love Jesus and the church;
to my sister, Meg,
for being my truest friend;
to my husband, Bobby,
for believing in me and cheering me on
to the finish line;
to my children, Hunter and Sarah Beth,
for bringing so much joy into my life.

112003

# Contents

# Contents

# Contents

Contents

## Contents

# Acknowledgments

My special thanks and appreciation to:

My husband, Bobby: for the years of support you have given me to pursue my dreams and for your hands-on help with the children while I was writing this book. You are the love of my life.

My children, Hunter and Sarah Beth: for being patient while I was working and interrupting me when it was time to have fun. I think you two are terrific.

My mom and dad, Trisha and Howard Edington: for giving me the idea for this book and adding valuable input along the way. I am proud to ride on your coattails.

My Sefton family, Meg, Billy, and Penn: for lots of play dates, hot meals, hurricane shelter (Charlie), and editing skills. You are family *and* dear friends.

My Hewitt family, Caren, Bob, Lisa, Scott, Endsley, Thomas, Hailey, and David: for encouraging words, hurricane shelter (Frances and Jeanne), computer support, and free babysitting. I am so thankful to be a part of your family.

My two great-grandmothers, GiGi and Nanny: for your inspiring lives and abiding faith. You are a blessing to me.

My church family in Selma, especially Becky and Jim: for back-porch fellowship and fanning to flame my passion for children's ministry. I treasure our friendship.

My First Presbyterian family in Orlando, especially Carol, Ted, and Tino: for all the creative teamwork. This book is the fruit of our ministry partnership.

My Grace Fellowship family in Orlando, especially Kelly and Mike: for giving our family a fresh start and a church to call home. I am so glad we are friends.

My girlfriends, Amy, Sara, Kim, Monique, Jennifer, and Paige: for your loving support and encouragement along the way. I thank God for you.

My agent, friend, and teacher, Robert Wolgemuth: for helping to bring this book to life. It wouldn't have happened without you.

Now to him who is able to do immeasurably more than all we ask or imagine, according to his power that is at work within us, to him be glory in the church and in Christ Jesus throughout all generations, for ever and ever! Amen.

Ephesians 3:20–21

# Part One

# The Power of the Children's Sermon

# 1

# Children in "Big Church"

What do children love to do? Think about it for a moment or two. What activities or situations naturally attract children? One of the first things I think of is water. Whether the water is gathered in a puddle in the street, shooting through a park fountain, or filled with bubbles in the bathtub, children love to play in water. How about ice cream? We do not have to teach children how to eat ice cream. They are born knowing how to squish it and shove it in their mouths. What about running? Put children at the end of a long hallway and off they go. Children love to run. Children love play-dough and paint and glue. Children love music and dancing. They love to jump and climb and wrestle, especially boys. They love using their imaginations. They love to watch themselves in the mirror. They love to talk and ask questions. They love to play with toys.

Several years ago, there was a commercial on television that illustrated how a child responds to something he loves.

The scene opens in the parents' bedroom. The parents are fast asleep. Suddenly, their son enters the bedroom, dressed for the day. He climbs onto the bed and starts shaking his parents by the shoulders as he tells them, "Wake up, wake up! You said you would take me to McDonald's today." The sleepy parents reach for the clock beside the bed to check the time. The father yawns and says, "Go back to bed, son. It's 3:00 in the morning." Now that is a child who loves McDonald's. He is up early. He dresses himself. He is ready to go.

It would be great if children responded to church this way. It would be great if children rose early on Sunday morning, jumped into their clothes, and woke their parents with the same enthusiasm as that boy in the McDonald's commercial: "Wake up, wake up! You said you would take me to church today." Just a dream? Maybe. But I want to make this point: There should be something about church that children love. I'm not just talking about Sunday school or the donuts at fellowship hour. I'm talking about something children anticipate in "big church," corporate worship, the gospel hour, revival time in the big tent—whatever you call it at your church.

Let's return to the McDonald's commercial for a moment. What is it about McDonald's that children love so much? Frankly, it is the children's menu: a child-sized burger or chicken nuggets, fries, a drink, and a *toy*. Fast-food restaurants have learned that children love something special just for them. Churches need to have something special just for kids in the context of worship. That is what the children's sermon is all about. It is a specialized children's message that is incorporated into the overall worship service.

If your church is not offering children's sermons during corporate worship, I hope this book will inspire you to add them. Children's sermons can endear children to the worship experience by making them feel welcomed and valued by their church family. But the ripple effects of great children's sermons extend beyond the hearts and minds of children. They can benefit the entire congregation.

*Children's sermons are a tangible way to show that children hold an important place in the kingdom of God.* Many churches say that children and families are important to their congregation, but they exclude or separate children from participating in the major activities of church life. Worship is one place this happens. In general, worship services are planned by adults for adults. Music selection, language, biblical text, and length of the sermon are all geared toward the adult heart, mind, and attention span. While a church would never advertise itself as "For Adults Only," that is how many worship services feel to children and their parents.

Since I am a preacher's daughter, I have many childhood memories of being in "big church." My sister, brother, and I were expected to sit still and listen to Dad's sermons. There were no special children's programs offered during the worship time. To my recollection, there was not even a children's bulletin or doodle pad to hold our attention. "Big church" was an adult-oriented place where children were expected to fit in. I remember my mom giving us candy midway through the service to help us get through. But other than that highlight, sitting through worship was something to be endured, not necessarily enjoyed. If children attended a worship service, they were expected to sit still and be quiet.

Today we know much more about how children grow and develop than we did thirty years ago. This knowledge has fueled a transformation in parenting, education, entertainment, and merchandising for children. Our society is full of child-sensitive environments and products. Children grow up in childproofed homes and travel from place to place in car seats or secured with seat belts. Toys are made for each stage of development to stimulate a child's brain while protecting the child from choking on small parts.

Entertainment parks specialize in creating the world at a child's eye level. Some hair salons feature carousel horses or pretend airplanes for children to sit in while getting their hair cut. Malls have indoor playgrounds. Grocery stores offer car-shaped shopping carts. More and more places creatively answer the question parents ask: "What do you offer that my children will like?"

It is time for the church to jump onto the child-friendly bandwagon, not only because modern society demands it but because Jesus modeled it. In the Bible we read the story of a group of parents who worked their way through a crowd of people to bring their children to meet Jesus face-to-face (Mark 10:13–16). They wanted Jesus to lay his hands on their children and bless them. Jesus was in the middle of a heated discussion about divorce with a suspicious group of Pharisees when the parents arrived. It was a tense situation. The subject matter certainly was not appropriate for young ears. As the parents pushed through the adults, getting their children closer and closer to Jesus, the disciples stopped them. They told the parents not to bother Jesus. He was busy. But Jesus overheard the disciples' reprimand and immediately shifted his focus from the Pharisees to the children and their parents. He bent down to scoop the children onto his lap. Then he proceeded to give the disciples, the Pharisees, and the crowd a minisermon of his own. He said: "Let the children come to me. Don't stop them! For the Kingdom of God belongs to such as these" (Mark 10:14 NLT). Scripture says that Jesus put his hands on the heads of the children and prayed for them.

In this story, Jesus demonstrates how important children are in the kingdom of God. It is a theme echoed throughout Scripture. It is interesting to note that the Bible records the childhood experiences of great men of faith such as Joseph, Moses, Samuel, and David. When these men were young, God was working in their lives to bring about his purposes.

Jesus said: "Whoever welcomes a little child like this in my name welcomes me. . . . See that you do not look down on one of these little ones. For I tell you that their angels in heaven always see the face of my Father in heaven" (Matt. 18:5, 10). Paul writes to young Timothy: "Don't let anyone think less of you because you are young. Be an example to all believers in what you teach, in the way you live, in your love, your faith, and your purity" (1 Tim. 4:12 NLT). From the biblical perspective, childhood is not merely a phase to pass through on the way to adulthood. Childhood is a time of divine purpose and meaning.

*Children's sermons give children an opportunity to teach adults.* Adults benefit from worshiping with children because children possess a kind of faith that is pleasing to God. They are quick to trust and believe. They are spontaneous. They are brutally honest. They are expressive. They are dependent. In *Transforming Children into Spiritual Champions*, George Barna states: "God enjoys the nature and personality of children. The Scriptures specifically identify attributes such as sincerity, humility, naiveté, vulnerability and simplicity as qualities found in children, and He treasures these characteristics."[1] When children are in worship and are given an opportunity to express themselves, adults have the opportunity to learn from them and emulate their childlike faith.

Here's an important goal to remember: Pleasing God is the aim of worship. And the worship of children is pleasing to God. So often, organized worship becomes more about what *we* need than what God deserves from us. We go to a worship service to be inspired, to recharge our batteries for the week ahead, and to find refuge from a world that is less and less tolerant of our beliefs and morals. With this distorted focus in worship, many adults feel that children detract and distract from the mood of worship. They talk at inappropriate moments. They squirm. They scribble noisily on the bulletin. Parents are often the ones who clamor the loudest for a child-free environment. Many of them see worship as an opportunity to get a break from parenting.

But worship is not about us and what we want. Worship is about God and what God wants. God desires the praises of his people—including children. It was God's plan that little babies and children would praise him. Psalm 8:2 says, "From the lips of children and infants you have ordained praise." If the involvement of children in worship is important to God, it should be important to us too.

*Finally, children's sermons provide a meaningful way to intentionally include children in the corporate worship experience.* Many churches offer alternative worship experiences just for children. "Children's church" can be popular with parents and children. But even with the most worshipful "children's church," there is still a hidden danger. If children never worship with adults during their formative years, how will they learn that "big church" is important and desirable? Ivy Beckwith asks: "If children are never included in our community worship rituals and practices, how will they ever learn to value them?"[2] She goes on to point out, "Worship is not only the time when the content of faith is delivered, but also the time when churches communicate the feelings, subtle nuances, and transcendent meanings of faith."[3] If children are isolated in their own worship experience, they will miss out on the community experience of their church family. Children's sermons provide a way to address the needs of children in an adult worship setting, thus preparing them for meaningful worship as adults.

We recently had a large portion of the sidewalk in front of our house replaced. My husband and I thought it would be neat to have our children put their hands in the wet cement to memorialize this stage in their lives. Unfortunately, the cement truck arrived while I was out running errands with the kids. When I pulled into our driveway and realized the cement had recently been poured, I threw the car into park, jumped out, and raced over to feel the surface. It was too late. The cement was damp to the touch, but the summer sun had already hardened it too much to leave an impression of any kind. How sad! What an opportunity missed!

When children are young, they are like newly poured cement. They are impressionable. This is why it is important to include children in corporate worship at a young age. Children who have meaningful worship experiences are more likely to value corporate worship when they mature into adulthood.

In the book *Spiritual Milestones*, the authors note that there are three general areas of child development. From birth to age seven, children are in the "imprint stage." At this time, children absorb everything we present to them. "What they believe about God during this time is mostly a reflection of what we [parents] believe."[4] From age seven to fifteen, children are in the "impression stage: [They] have the greatest receptivity to our values and beliefs, with the *potential* of taking up these beliefs as their very own. . . . Children begin to seek their spiritual identity during this time, and we need to seize the opportunity when it exists."[5] After age fifteen, teens are in the "coach stage" and are much less receptive to our Christian values and beliefs about worship.[6] They are more likely to test and challenge the things they have been taught. These insights teach us that we need to incorporate children into "big church" when they are young enough to still be receptive to our values and beliefs about worship. If we wait until children enter adolescence, we may have missed a crucial opportunity to teach them that worship is important.

When I was a little girl sitting in the pew on Sunday mornings, one quiet game I played was counting how many people around me had white hair. Then I would count the gray-headed people. Finally, I would add up how many people wore glasses. I perfected my technique enough to hold my head still and just move my eyes from side to side, up and down the rows of people. It was a way to keep myself occupied during the worship service. In the long run, this simple game taught me more than that. It taught me that the presence of older adults is crucial for a healthy congregation. Older adults bring a maturity of faith, a depth of experience, and an abiding sense of history that is pivotal to a church's sense of identity.

Now, as a children's ministry director and a mother of two young children, when I look up and down the pews on Sunday mornings, I am looking for the blonde curls and the brown cowlicks of children interspersed between the white- and gray-haired adults. The presence of children is also crucial for a healthy congregation. Children bring a freshness of faith, an excitement about life, and a glimpse into the future that invigorates an entire church family. Children have an important place in the pew with adults. It is our responsibility to make them feel like they belong.

# 2

# Buy One, Get One Free

The grocery store where I do my shopping offers weekly "buy one, get one free" specials. One week, if you buy a bottle of ketchup at the regular price, you get another bottle of the same kind of ketchup for free. The next week, it might be cereal: Buy one box; get a second box for free. You do not need to use coupons or present a discount card. It is a simple, straightforward way to save money. Since I am the main shopper, lunch fixer, snack provider, and short-order cook in our house, I get really excited about these specials.

There is a powerful "buy one, get one free" effect inherent in great children's messages. The target participants in the children's message are the children. But since the children's sermon takes place in the middle of a sanctuary full of adults, grown-ups get a message thrown in for free. In my ten years of leading children's sermons in worship, I can testify to the fact that adult worshipers are listening and learning right along with the children. I know because many adults have told me so.

Children's sermons appeal to adults for three reasons. First of all, they are easy to remember. A good children's sermon seeks to communicate one main point in approximately five minutes. A short message is more easily remembered in its entirety than a twenty- to thirty-minute sermon from the pulpit. A good children's sermon often includes a prop or some other creative activity that grabs the attention of both children and adults and leaves a lasting impression. Biblical language and wording can be difficult to understand. A good children's sermon translates these complexities into simple sentences children and adults can easily comprehend. Just because someone is an adult does not mean that he or she is biblically literate or even familiar with church lingo. Children's sermons are a respectful way to communicate basic Bible stories and concepts to all ages without babying or embarrassing anyone.

Second, children's sermons reconnect adults with their own childhood. They give adults an opportunity to be kids again. In his book *Let the Children Come*, Brant Baker writes: "We could say that everyone who sits in the congregation is nothing more than a grown-up child. That part of us isn't content to just sit and watch: we want to play, too. Children's sermons offer the consummate intergenerational teaching experience."[1]

I have used one of Brant Baker's children's sermons about parting the Red Sea on several different occasions.[2] In this children's sermon, the children are the Israelites; they are in back of the sanctuary. The congregation is the Red Sea. The adults stand up and move into the aisle until there is a solid wall of people. On Moses's command (played by a child volunteer), the Red Sea parts (adults move back into the pews to create an open pathway), allowing the Israelites to walk through on dry ground (children move through the congregation to the front of the sanctuary).

But just as the Israelites make it to the other shore of the Red Sea, they notice the Egyptian army (church ushers wielding garden hoes, rakes, golf clubs, and other "weapons") in hot pursuit. Moses gives the signal again; the waters of the Red Sea close in on the Egyptian army (adults move back into the aisle to stop the army), and the army is swept away by the water. God has rescued the Israelites in a miraculous way.

This creative retelling of a familiar biblical story ignites the whole congregation. Adults, who normally sit quietly through worship, relish the chance to play an active part in the story for the sake of the children. I've seen adults do the wave for Noah's ark, "baa" like sheep for the Christmas story, bop giant beach balls around the sanctuary, and learn sign language to simple Bible verses right along with the children.

Third, children's sermons model spiritual training for parents who are in the congregation. The Bible teaches us that God intends for parents to be the primary spiritual educators of their children. Faith is passed from one generation to the next, not so much during an hour of worship on Sunday but in the context of everyday family life. The church plays a vital but secondary role to parents in the spiritual nurture of children.

Sundays are a time for parents to be spiritually renewed and encouraged as they seek to raise their children to know, love, and live for Jesus Christ. During a children's sermon, parents can observe how biblical truths are communicated to children. They have the opportunity to watch another adult explain theological concepts in an age-appropriate way or struggle to answer children's seemingly endless questions about weighty matters of faith. The goal is not to "wow" parents with perfect presentations and content; the goal is to make talking to children about God feel normal, natural, and doable for Christian parents.

My children's sermon one Sunday was about what freedom means to Christians. I talked about the fact that freedom is not the absence of rules. Freedom is given to us through Christ as we obey his rules and live the right way. To make the point, I tied up a child from head to toe to show how sin, disobeying God's rules, traps us instead of setting us free. The mother of the boy I tied up spoke to me after worship. She said, "I am so glad you gave this message today. We have been struggling with our son at home. He is bucking all of our family rules. We just had a conversation with him about it this morning. Now I can use this lesson to remind him of what God's rules really do in our lives." Equipping parents with biblical truths that relate to the life of their child is an added bonus of children's sermons.

To further support adults in their spiritual parenting, it is effective to provide a take-home component with children's sermons. If the topic of the children's sermon is the importance of reading the Bible, then give parents a handout about how to read the Bible with their children at home and what children's Bibles your church recommends. The "Bugs in the Bible" (see p. 95) and "A Bible Verse for Life" (see p. 85) children's sermons in this book are designed to spill over into the home by giving parents specific tasks to accomplish with their children around Bible study and memorizing Bible verses. For the "Christmas Night Live" series (see pp. 161–73), we found nativity scene window clings with a home devotional to distribute to our families. During the "Back to School Blessing" (see p. 139), parents are asked to directly participate with their children in the children's sermon. Give parents information about the biblical concept of blessings with a few ideas for blessings they can try at home. The worship bulletin is a great place to "advertise" your children's sermons and provide brief, helpful spiritual training information for parents.

As we have seen, children's sermons have the *potential* to stimulate the entire congregation. This does not happen automatically, however. Going through the motions does not insure success. Children's sermons can be boring, confusing, or fluffy fun with no solid content. To deliver a children's sermon with intergenerational impact, you have to create a point of intersection between the developmental characteristics of children and relevant biblical content. A good children's sermon speaks directly to children about matters of faith in a way they can understand and assimilate into their daily lives. It captures their attention. It touches on experiences they face. It answers questions they ask. It makes the Bible real and relevant. To do this well, you have to know where children are coming from, what interests them, and how they think. Here are some developmental characteristics of children that directly relate to the development of effective children's sermons.

*Children are concrete and literal thinkers.* They do not fully understand abstract concepts or symbolic language. Developmental psychologists and educators agree that children are not able to think abstractly until late childhood, between the ages of twelve and fourteen. Since most children who participate in children's sermons are younger than twelve, it is important to use concrete language and say exactly what you mean to teach biblical truth. This can be particularly challenging because so much of the Bible contains abstract concepts and principles. Phrases such as "God is love," "The Lord is my shepherd," or "Jesus is the light of the world" are all abstract principles subject to misinterpretation by children.

Jesus encountered a similar challenge in communicating spiritual concepts to his disciples. One example of this can be found in John 4:31–34. The disciples encouraged Jesus to have something to eat. Part of their job was to tend to the Master's needs. The disciples must have been concerned about Jesus's physical stamina. But he said to them: "I have food to eat that you know nothing about" (v. 32). This baffled the disciples. They said to themselves, "Could someone have brought him food?" (v. 33); they were still thinking in concrete terms. To them, food was a piece of fish or a barley loaf. But Jesus meant something different by the word *food*. Jesus was talking about the sustenance and nourishment that come from following God's will. He said, "My food is to do the will of him who sent me and to finish his work" (v. 34). Jesus was speaking in abstract terms about food.

To communicate clearly with children, we need to use words in their concrete terms. Food means a peanut butter and jelly sandwich. Instead of asking children if they face a "Goliath" problem, we ask them, "What is something big that you worry about?"

On the other hand, just because children have a hard time understanding abstract thought and language does not mean that we avoid it altogether. Love is an abstract concept we use with children all the time. As parents, we constantly tell our little ones "I love you" as we hold them, rock them, and kiss them. Our loving actions linked with the words "I love you" teach children what love means. Ivy Beckwith explains:

> In order to enable young children to understand abstract concepts, parents and teachers need to link them to something concrete and do it every time the action happens or the concept is discussed. . . . Each time a concrete action is linked to an abstract concept the child is closer to understanding the larger idea.[3]

In addition to linking abstract ideas with concrete actions, we need to define abstract words in language that children understand. If you are talking to children about sin, use the word *sin* and then define it as well. For example, you may say, "Sin is disobeying God's rules." To repent means to stop doing what is wrong and start doing what is right. At Easter, when you talk about the resurrection, define the word. *Resurrection* means "coming back to life again." In crafting age-appropriate children's sermons, you cannot assume that children know the definitions of the theological terms you are using. You must take a brief moment to define your abstract words to be sure children understand what you are trying to teach them.

*Children use their whole bodies to learn.* Children love to move. They like to touch things, taste things, smell things, and see things. They like to *do*—to actively participate. These are not methods we traditionally associate with corporate worship. Most worship involves standing, sitting, singing, maybe some kneeling, and a whole lot of listening. Sitting and listening rank low on the list of children's favorite activities. Therefore, we should limit sitting and listening activities for children in church. A good children's sermon capitalizes on the ways children learn best—through movement and sensory experience.

My husband and I were teaching preschool Sunday school recently. The children were happily playing at the various learning centers. As the time for our Bible story approached, I gave the class the warning that it was almost time to clean up the room to get ready for the Bible story. Ben, a three-year-old boy, said to me, "I don't want to sit and listen to a Bible story." I responded: "But, Ben, you are not going to sit and listen. We are all going to act out the story together." His eyes got wide with excitement as he joined in the cleanup effort so we could get to the Bible story. That morning, we pretended to be the Israelite army who was afraid to fight Goliath, played by my husband, as we hid behind the tables in the classroom. Then we imagined that we were brave like David because we trusted in God. We faced Goliath and pretended to swing our slingshots over our heads, around and around, until the imaginary stone flew out to hit Goliath in the head. The Bible story came to life.

The same should be true in corporate worship. The children's sermon is a time for the Bible to come to life for children. Many of the scripted children's sermons in this book get children moving. Whether it's racing around the sanctuary, acting out Psalm 139, climbing a ladder, or playing a game of tug-of-war, movement insures that children are engaged participants instead of dull-eyed observers. One Valentine's Day Sunday, the children helped to share God's love with others by passing out heart-shaped balloons to the congregation. At Christmastime, I have used the children to create a human Advent wreath. We have also put on crowns and traveled from the east (the narthex) to the stable (the chancel) just like the wise men did when they were searching for the baby Jesus. Let me say, this is not just movement for movement's sake. We are not just playacting at church. We are communicating the gospel in a way that connects with the hearts and minds of children.

*Children have short attention spans.* A general rule of thumb is that children have one minute of attention span for each year of life. A five-year-old has an attention span of five minutes. This means that children's sermons should be short and simple. Great messages follow the "get in, get to the point, get out" principle. The leader "gets in" by quickly capturing the children's attention. Then the leader "gets to the point" by sharing the Bible concept and carefully linking it to everyday life for children. A short prayer is the best way to "get out." We must resist the temptation to lecture on and on to children, to read long passages of Scripture, or make more than one important point about a Bible story. This means that leaders of children's sermons must carefully prepare what they are going to say, being sure to streamline Bible stories and Scripture passages to capture their essence, not necessarily their entirety. More is not more in the world

32

of communicating with children. The longer we talk, the less children listen and remember.

The story of Jesus blessing the children illustrates the challenges and benefits of ministering to both adults and children at the same time (Mark 10:13–16). To the disciples, the children were interrupting Jesus as he dealt with issues in the adult world. To Jesus, the children were a welcome reminder of what the kingdom of God is all about. Instead of ignoring the children or rescheduling a separate time to meet with them, Jesus stopped what he was doing, gave them his undivided attention for a few moments, and then moved on. I love the thought of Jesus bending down to the level of the children to pull them into his arms and bless them while the adults stand by watching and listening. It is a snapshot of effective interplay between generations. It models why children's sermons are so effective for the whole congregation.

33

# 3

Priming the Pump
for Great Ideas

An ancient Chinese proverb reads: "Give a man a fish, and you feed him for a day. Teach a man to fish, and you feed him for a lifetime." This book *gives* you fifty field-tested children's sermons you can use in your church right away. But more than that, this book is designed to *teach* you how to develop a lifetime of great children's sermons on your own.

A great children's message begins with a great idea. But where do great ideas come from? One source for ideas is the content of the adult sermon. In a perfect world, the children's sermon and the adult sermon in the worship service should complement one another. When I am preparing a children's sermon, the first question I ask is, "What is the topic and biblical text of the adult sermon?" If the topic and biblical text are appropriate for children,

I develop a child's version of the adult message. These complementary sermons synergize the worship service for the whole congregation.

One of the joys of my life in ministry has been to serve on the church staff with my father. For eight years, Dad was the senior minister and I was the director of children's ministry. Those years of teamwork taught me the value of connecting the children's sermon with the adult sermon. During the Advent season, Dad planned a series of sermons entitled "Faces at the Manger" that touched on the different characters in the first Christmas story. Following his lead, I worked with my team to develop the "Christmas Night Live" series (see pp. 161–73) for the children, teaching the children about the same characters in a more condensed format. Around the Fourth of July, Dad preached a sermon on the theme of God and country. My children's sermon was "What Freedom Means" (see p. 157). When Dad preached about "Four Men in the Fiery Furnace," the children acted out the story of Shadrach, Meshach, and Abednego during the children's sermon (see p. 76).

Those years of teamwork also taught me important principles for adapting children's sermons from the adult sermon. First of all, the adult sermon is often multifaceted, containing several main ideas. The corresponding children's message should deal with one main idea. You should pick the most salient message to be communicated to the children. Second, Bible stories and text that are appropriate for adults need to be condensed and edited for children. This often means leaving out details and skipping genealogies or peripheral characters that are not essential to the main story line. In other instances, you will need to omit or tone down any subject matter (such as sexual content or violence) that is not suitable for young ears. It is always a good idea to briefly define terms or cultural traditions that may be unfamiliar to children as you go along. These guidelines will help you create a child-sized portion of the adult sermon.

On the other hand, there are times when it does not make sense to use the adult sermon as the basis for the children's sermon. Sometimes the topic for the sermon is not relevant to the lives of children. Other times, there is a burning issue in the lives of children that does not affect adults in the same way—such as the start of a new school year. In these instances, it is more important to address the specific needs of the children than to connect the message of the children's sermon with the adult sermon.

## Children's Sermons That Stand on Their Own

To brainstorm ideas for children's sermons that stand on their own, I ask myself the following questions:

What Bible story can I tell?
What biblical concept do children need to understand and apply to their lives?
What prop can I use to teach a spiritual truth?
What event in the lives of children can I relate to the Bible?
What children's sermons series can I create to teach a multifaceted subject?

In the remaining pages of this chapter, you will see how to use these questions to craft creative children's sermons.

### Story-Driven Ideas

Children love good stories. Thankfully, the Bible is full of them. Contrary to what some children may have experienced at church, Bible stories are *not* boring. Some of the juiciest stories of all time are found in Scripture. The way we tell Bible stories to children should be as captivating as the stories themselves.

Children are quickly turned off by long, complicated stories read directly from the Bible. The best way to tell Bible stories to children is to say to them, "Today I am going to tell you an awesome story from the Bible, and I need your help." Getting children actively involved in telling Bible stories chases boredom right out of the sanctuary. This participation can take a variety of forms. Children can act out the story. They can make sound effects. They can hold props. They can wear costumes. They can repeat words or phrases from the story. When you give children something to do in the Bible story, they will listen and learn.

In addition, select Bible stories that are interesting to children. I use children's Bible story books and Sunday school curriculum outlines to help guide me in what is age-appropriate for children. Bible stories that include children and animals are naturally interesting to children. Children also love Bible stories about miracles. Look for stories that convey action and emotion.

Once the story is selected, edit the story to fit the context of your worship space and the time constraints of the children's sermon. Sometimes this means you will need to leave out details or background information of the story that would take too much time to explain. Even short Bible stories can be open to many interpretations. Resist the temptation to say too much about the various meanings of a story by choosing one main point you want to communicate.

Although you do not want to read an entire story directly from the Bible, it is important that children know the story you are telling comes from the Bible, not just from your imagination. You can do this by having a Bible with you as you tell the story. Open the Bible to the place where the story is written. Share the Bible reference with the children. You may even add a statement such as: "Today's story comes from the book of Genesis in the Bible. We know this is a true story, because all of the stories in the Bible are true."

## Concept-Driven Ideas

The apostle Paul wrote to the Romans: "Don't copy the behavior and customs of this world, but let God transform you into a new person by changing the way you think" (Rom. 12:2 NLT). Just as in Paul's day, the values of our postmodern world stand in sharp contrast to our Christian values. The children in our churches today are growing up in a society that increasingly rejects absolute, objective truth. Given this cultural challenge, we must be more intentional about passing on biblical truth to our children and connecting that truth to their everyday lives. Concept-driven children's sermons are one way to do this.

Instead of starting with a Bible story, these children's sermons start with a biblical concept to be taught to children. In "A Lesson from Copernicus" (see p. 91), the concept children are taught is the purpose of life. The world teaches us to be self-centered in our approach to life. Life is about what we want and what we have. As Christians, our lives are to be God-centered. The purpose of our lives is to show that God is great and to submit to what he wants. In "A Servant Attitude" (see p. 93), the world's definition of greatness is contrasted with the actions of the greatest person to ever live—Jesus Christ. Jesus showed us how true greatness is determined: not by money, possessions, or popularity but by how we serve God and other people.

My son recently saw a commercial for cereal on television. He begged me to buy him the cereal. On my next trip to the grocery store, I purchased what I thought was the cereal he saw advertised. I proudly presented it to my son when I returned home. Instead of a joyful "Yippee!"

he moaned, "Mom, that's not the right cereal. The cereal I want is the kind that makes you smile and laugh all day long. That's what the commercial said." Now I was the one laughing. I tried to explain that there is no such thing as a cereal that makes you smile and laugh all day long. He wasn't buying it. He sulked out of the kitchen with tears in his eyes. After comforting him, I thought to myself, *This would make a great children's sermon!* Commercials on television tell us we can buy things that will make us happy. The Bible teaches us that true fulfillment can be found in God alone (see Isa. 55:2 and Ps. 63:3–5).

To generate your own ideas for concept-driven children's sermons, use a topical Bible to make a list of concepts with related Bible verses connected with the everyday life of children. These concepts might include love, forgiveness, sharing, possessions, friendship, money, fear, anger, envy, obedience, truth, discipline, work, temptation, loneliness, prayer, heaven, and death. Come up with an example of how the world defines each of these concepts, and then compare and contrast the world's idea with biblical truth. Finally, give an example of how biblical truth works in everyday life.

## Prop-Driven Ideas

Using props is one of the best ways to get children to pay attention to what you are saying. Children like to see objects that relate to what they are learning. If they can touch the props, that is even better. You will find that most of the children's sermons in this book use props in one way or another. I rarely do a children's sermon empty-handed.

A prop-driven children's sermon starts with an object—such as play-dough, a tug-of-war rope, a ladder, a pumpkin—and uses that object to point the way to a spiritual truth. A prop can be an actual object that is mentioned in the Bible text, such as a tent in "Earthly Tents and Heavenly Homes" (see p. 117). Or the prop can be something not directly mentioned in the story or text but that relates a spiritual truth in some concrete way. Costumes, hats, toys, drawings, food, musical instruments, and cue cards all make great props. Any object that creates a good visual representation of the concept you are trying to teach is a good prop.

Caution: Props can get out of control. If you're not careful, props can take over the children's sermon. One Sunday, to illustrate how God protects us, I played some storm sound effects and opened up four large golf umbrellas. I asked the children to gather under the umbrellas. They complied nicely. But that was the last time they listened to a word I said. As the children huddled in their own little umbrella worlds, they were so excited to be there that they started chattering and giggling out loud. Soon they were arguing about who was going to hold the umbrella next and swapping storm stories with one another. Since they were under the large umbrellas and I was not, I could not make eye contact with them to get their attention. My repeated attempts to get them to stop talking and listen went unheeded. I started to break out into a sweat. There was nervous laughter from the congregation. I finally admitted, "I've lost control!" as I took the umbrellas back from the children and mumbled a quick closing prayer. I will never use umbrellas again.

Just as spices are meant to flavor food without overwhelming the taste of the main ingredient, good props add flavor to a children's sermon without distracting from the message. To insure the desired effects of a prop, follow these guidelines:

1. *Keep props simple.* You will feel more confident using props if they are not too complicated to operate, hold, or manipulate.

2. *Test props to be sure they will work.* Just because you read about an idea for a science experiment or other object lesson in a book does not mean it will work for you. Try it for yourself first.

3. *Practice using props in front of a mirror.* You want to be sure you hold your prop in such a way that everyone can see it and see you too.

4. *Decide ahead of time if you need someone to help you with the props.* You can line up an adult helper in advance or recruit children to help you on the spot.

5. *Make sure props are the right size for your worship space.* If you are in a big sanctuary with a lot of children, the scale of props should be large. If you are in a smaller space, you can use smaller-sized objects.

6. *Have a backup plan in case a prop backfires.* What will you say to the children and the congregation if your prop doesn't work? It is not the end of the world, but you do need to have an exit strategy in case it happens.

### Event-Driven Ideas

Another great way to generate creative ideas for children's sermons is to link biblical truth with the major events in the lives of children. There are certain times of year that are very important to children. These include the start of school, birthdays, Christmas, and the beginning of summer. Look for stories and Scripture that can help children navigate these benchmark experiences.

As I was writing this book, we were in the midst of a busy hurricane season in Florida. Our state was hit by four separate hurricanes within the course of two months. In our city, schools were shut down, sporting events were canceled, and houses lost power. Our church canceled worship services one Sunday because a hurricane was making landfall that day. The first Sunday we were back in church,

I felt I had to talk with the children about their hurricane experiences. I brought my hurricane supplies out during the children's sermon time and talked about how the Bible can help us prepare for bad weather. I handed out "Hurricane Preparation Bible Verses" for the children to put in their box of hurricane supplies at home. This is an example of how to link children's experiences to scriptural principles about trusting God and praying when you are afraid.

Event-driven children's sermons have the power to make God's Word relevant in the everyday lives of children. For many children, the Bible seems antiquated. It was written so long ago. It contains words and names and places that are hard for children to understand without the help of adults. It is probably the longest book children will ever be encouraged to read. Therefore, whenever we can directly connect the Bible to current events in children's lives, we teach them that God's Word can help them understand life today.

### Series-Driven Ideas

One of the best ways to gather momentum from creative ideas is to develop a series of children's sermons over the course of several weeks. Children learn more when lessons are reviewed and reinforced from week to week. The layering effect of adding one lesson on top of another helps children develop a comprehensive understanding of complex stories or concepts.

Series-driven sermons work particularly well around the seasons of Advent and Lent, but they can be used anytime during the year with some planning in advance. Here are some ideas for series-driven sermons:

- "Something's Fishy"—Bible stories having to do with fish of any shape or size. Dress up like a fisherman to tell the stories.

- "Hark and Harold"—two Christmas angels who make advance preparations on earth for the birth of Jesus. Where will the baby be born? Who will the parents be? Who will receive the birth announcements?
- "Back to School Countdown"—issues children face as they go back to school. Deal with one topic per week: Obeying Your Teacher, Doing Your Homework, Receiving Report Cards, Making Friends.
- "Bible Safari"—action-packed Bible stories involving animals. Make cutouts of each animal; have people dress in animal costumes or bring animal masks that the children can wear. What do the animal stories teach us about God and/or people?

Although series-driven sermons require a good deal of advance preparation, they bring a unique energy and sense of anticipation to the children's sermon time. They arouse children's curiosity. When children ask, "What are you going to do next week?" you can respond, "You'll just have to come back to church and find out for yourself!"

I believe creativity is a trait we all inherit from our Creator God. No one person or personality type has the corner on the creativity market. The potential for creativity exists in all of us. The five approaches for children's sermons outlined in this chapter can help stretch and strengthen your creativity muscle. In addition to these approaches, I encourage you to find two or three people who are passionate about children's ministry and are willing to brainstorm children's sermon ideas with you. This group process can transform your good ideas into an awesome final product. Creativity thrives in group settings. Finally, pass all your creative ideas through the reality filter. The next chapter will give you the information you need to turn your creative ideas into children's sermons that work in the real world.

# 4

## Preparing for Children's Sermon Success

I learned the most important lessons about children's sermons not so much from my graduate school training or early years as a Christian educator but from watching my father prepare and deliver his sermons. Like most ministers, Dad spends a large portion of his ministry hours preparing sermons for Sunday mornings. He has a detailed system for developing a yearly sermon schedule, monthly research and writing time, and weekly in-depth preparation. Because of his disciplined approach to sermon preparation, he delivers thought-provoking and passionate sermons completely from memory week after week. Although children's sermons certainly require much less work than it takes to develop adult sermons, my father taught me that good preparation is the key to delivering great sermons.

*To prepare a great children's sermon, you need time to develop creative ideas and communication techniques.* Saturday night is too late to dream about eye-catching props or elaborate scenery for your children's sermon the next day. The more time you can give yourself to pray for God's guidance, do some in-depth study, and brainstorm ideas, the more likely you are to come up with a creative children's sermon. I try to get a topic in mind at least two weeks in advance. I keep it in the back of my mind as I go about my other work. I jot down any ideas that come to me. Then I set a definite time one week in advance to make a rough outline and begin gathering necessary supplies. On Wednesday or Thursday before I am giving the Sunday children's sermon, I write out a script in detail. Over the years, I have found that writing out exactly what I am going to say insures that I say things clearly and concisely. Since children's sermons are short, I cannot afford to ramble on or beat around the bush. The discipline of writing a script helps me to make every word count. Finally, I spend Saturday memorizing the script and practicing it out loud so I am ready to deliver my children's sermon from memory on Sunday morning.

Adequate lead time also makes it possible to get other people to help you with your children's sermons. I have relied on people in the congregation to build props, draw pictures, sew costumes, tie balloons, and assemble goodie bags for the children to take home. To delegate tasks and share the workload inevitable in a creative children's sermon, you have to be respectful of other people's time. That means staying several weeks ahead of schedule so you are not asking for last-minute help. Being on time can also save you money. I often order props or take-home elements through catalogs or the Internet. Waiting until the last minute to purchase supplies often costs more money. There are also local vendors who will donate food, printing services, or other items with advance notice.

Series-driven children's sermons require the most advance planning. A good rule of thumb is to follow the planning strategy of retailers. When the Fourth of July is over, stores immediately put out back-to-school supplies. After the first day of school, Halloween jack-o'-lanterns and costumes fill the aisles. By early October, lights, ornaments, and Christmas decorations are everywhere! Use this same seasonal approach in your children's sermon planning. This means a series of Christmas children's sermons should be planned in early fall. You should begin brainstorming for Easter ideas by the end of January.

At this point, you may be thinking I am going a bit overboard about children's sermon preparation. Maybe this sounds like a lot of unnecessary work and attention for such a small part of a worship service. I believe that if children's sermons are worth doing in corporate worship, they are worth doing well. Sunday worship is "prime time" in the life of the church. Children, parents, church leaders, and other adults are assembled as a captive audience for a taste of children's ministry each week. This is an amazing opportunity to communicate the excitement of the gospel message to little ones, inspire parents, and build congregational support for ministry to children all at once. I would encourage you to roll up your sleeves, turn on your creative juices, and put some time and energy into creating children's sermons that really make a difference in the way your church worships together.

*To prepare a great children's sermon, you also need to be ready for the spontaneous antics of children.* In a Sunday school setting, you can continually review basic classroom rules with children. You can put down carpet squares for children to sit on during story time to keep them from sitting on each other. You can quietly separate children who are talking with each other or fighting over a toy. If all else fails, you can pull out juice and crackers and have snack time. In a worship setting, directing the behavior of children is a unique challenge.

First, children from the ages of two to twelve may come forward for the children's sermon. This broad range of ages breeds diverse behavior. Older children are generally accustomed to listening to a teacher in a group setting. For younger children, a children's sermon may be a brand-new experience. Second, when children come forward for the children's sermon, they often sense that they are in the limelight. This can result in two extremes of behavior. Being in a crowd makes some children feel shy and clingy. Other children, however, relish the thought of being in front of an audience. They make silly faces, talk out loud, mimic your expressions, or wave to their parents. The congregation can exacerbate the situation by laughing at the funny things children say or do. The spontaneous behavior and energy of children are certainly part of the appeal of including them in worship. However, there are some important things to do to keep the behavior of children and the response of the congregation from overwhelming the message of the children's sermon.

I recommend inviting parents to come forward with their children for the children's sermon. Parents can either sit with their children or they can sit close by. You need some adults scattered among the children to help with crowd control. When a child is talking out loud, standing up and waving, or wrestling with a friend, an adult sitting nearby can gently get the child's attention and redirect his or her behavior while you continue with your message.

On Easter Sunday, a two-year-old boy named Carter came forward for his first children's sermon. He was excited to be there. He stood up and waved to his mom who was sitting in the congregation. Then, as I started my message, Carter kept asking his mom out loud, "Where's Daddy? Where's Daddy?" Thankfully, his daddy was sitting close by. I stopped what I was doing and helped Carter find his daddy. From the security of his daddy's lap, Carter participated beautifully with the rest of the children in the children's sermon. This is one of the benefits of having parents close by their children during this special worship time.

I also think it is important to get the children to sit close to me. If children are spread out across the front of the sanctuary, I ask them to move in closer before I get started. The closer children are to the action, the more likely they are to pay attention. I like to make good eye contact with them or even reach out and touch the shoulder of a child who may appear distracted.

If a child does interrupt or act out during the children's sermon and there is no adult close by to help out, I try not to get rattled or upset. Children are on a learning curve when it comes to being able to control their behavior. It is normal for them to misbehave from time to time. If a child talks when I am talking, and nonverbal cues are not working, I might calmly say, "John, it is my turn to talk. I need you to listen." If a child wants to share a long, personal story right in the middle of the children's sermon, I might say, "Jennifer, I would love to hear your story after we are finished. Right now, I need you to listen to me." Then I would be sure to catch up with Jennifer after the church service to listen carefully to her story. On the rare occasion when a child is so disruptive that the other children are no longer paying attention, stop the children's sermon, calmly ask for help from a parent or another adult, wait for the child to be removed from the group, and then finish your message.

Over the years, I have worked with some children who are particularly activated by children's sermons. They quickly learn that they can get a laugh by praying too loudly or asking silly questions or just being goofy in front of the congregation. While causing the congregation to laugh is harmless from time to time, the children's sermon is not a weekly entertainment show. Allowing this dynamic to pervade the worship service is ultimately disrespectful to the children and to God. If a child is repeatedly acting out during the children's sermon, I call the child's parents at home and talk with them about the situation. The goal is not to quench a child's spirit but to direct his or her behavior in ways that are appropriate for the context of worship.

*To prepare a great children's sermon, you need to be efficient with your time.* By this, I mean you need to have an action plan that keeps things moving quickly so your children's sermons keep the attention of the children. Setting up props, selecting volunteers, and passing out materials can be time wasters. Careful planning can streamline these activities.

I often recruit people to help me carry props or dress children in costumes. A helper can be doing the prep work while I am instructing the children about what we are going to do in the children's sermon. If I need children to volunteer to do a special task in the children's sermon, I often recruit them in advance. If I have to pass out something to the children to use during the children's sermon, I usually do this as the children are coming forward. Again, other helpers speed up this process.

If something has to be given out for the children to take home, you can use helpers to pass out the materials after the prayer or you can pass them out as the children leave the sanctuary at the end of worship. In our church, children leave worship after the children's sermon to go to Sunday school. To save time in worship, I give take-home materials to the Sunday school teachers to pass out to the children. This kind of streamlining insures that the majority of time in worship is devoted to teaching instead of setting up props or distributing materials.

*Finally, to be prepared means to be ready for the unexpected.* Sunday morning worship is like live television—

anything can happen, and the show must go on. By thinking through some possible scenarios in advance, you can avoid panicking or freezing up if you get thrown a curveball in the middle of a children's sermon.

For example, what will you do if a prop that forms the centerpiece of your children's sermon doesn't work right? I once did a children's sermon that called for a child to try to hit a ball with a bat while wearing a blindfold. I was trying to make the point that you have to keep your eyes on the ball to hit it well, just like Peter needed to keep his eyes on Jesus when he was walking on the water (see Matt. 14:22–33). The problem occurred when the blindfolded child swung the bat and forcefully hit the ball. Maybe it was luck, or maybe this child was a gifted baseball player, but it ruined the point I was trying to make. What would you do if this happened to you?

What would you do if a child got sick in the middle of your children's sermon? It may be unpleasant to think about, but it can happen. Do you have cleaning supplies nearby? What would you say to the other children? Would you continue with your children's sermon, or would you pray for the child who is sick?

One Sunday morning, I woke up with laryngitis. I could not speak above a whisper. There was no one else to take my place. It was the quietest children's sermon I have ever delivered. Do you have a backup plan in case you get sick or have a family emergency? It is a great idea to have a fully scripted children's sermon that requires no supplies on file at the church. In a pinch, another staff person or volunteer could quickly read through the script that morning and give the children's sermon.

What if the child misbehaving during the children's sermon is your own? My daughter is in a phase right now where she gets very shy and clingy when I am leading the children's sermon. Thankfully, my husband holds her on his lap far enough away from the action that she feels comfortable. If you have children who participate in worship, are there issues you might face as you lead the children's sermon? Parenting your child while you are teaching other children can be awkward. Enlist the help of your spouse or another parent if your children need special attention while you are leading worship.

Perhaps the most important strategy in dealing with the unexpected is to maintain a sense of humor. Brant Baker writes: "The ability to laugh, with the children and at oneself, will go a long way in defusing some of the more outrageous things that inevitably *will* happen."[1] If your children's sermons are interrupted by an embarrassing situation that makes everyone laugh, laugh with them. Children will learn important lessons about grace and humility and what it means to be part of a church family by the way you navigate these zany moments.

Finally, let me say a word about preparing your heart for children's sermons. For many years, giving children's sermons has been a part of my job. I feel a professional responsibility for my part in worship on Sunday mornings. At the same time, leading children's sermons is a holy opportunity. I feel responsible for teaching children God's Word in a way that is pleasing to him. I hope that children will understand God more clearly and love him more deeply as a result of what they experience during the children's sermon. My favorite moments of preparation take place on Sunday mornings before the worship service as our worship team huddles together for prayer. Each of us has a different role within the worship service, so this prayer time helps us focus on honoring and magnifying God together. I encourage you to prepare your heart through prayer before you lead children in worship. Beyond all the colorful props, crazy costumes, and creative techniques, great children's sermons are about glorifying God.

# Part Two

# Children's Sermons You Can Do

# 5

## Story-Driven Children's Sermons

### A Handful of Thanks

**Bible Texts:** Luke 17:11–19; James 1:17

**Message:** We must thank God for the good things he does for us.

**Preparation:** None

**Script:** We are going to use our hands to tell a Bible story this morning. Put both your hands in the air and wiggle your fingers to get them warmed up. Now we're ready. I want you to do whatever I do with my hands.

One day Jesus was traveling to Jerusalem. (*Slowly walk two of your fingers.*) He was passing by a small village when he heard some men cry out to him. (*Put a hand to your ear as if you are listening.*) There were ten men. Count with me: 1, 2, 3, 4, . . . 9, 10 (*hold up your fingers as you count*). These ten men cried out (*cup your hands to your mouth*), "Jesus, Master, have mercy on us!"

You see, these ten men (*hold up ten fingers*) had a disease called leprosy. It is a skin disease that causes painful sores all over the body. (*Gently rub one hand on the other.*) These men had to live outside the village (*push both hands away from you*), away from their friends and family, because it was very easy to catch leprosy from someone who had the disease.

Jesus called back to the men with leprosy (*cup your hands to your mouth*), "Go and find a priest in the village and show him you are well." The men must have thought it was a strange thing for Jesus to say, because when they looked down at their hands (*look down at your hands*), they still saw the painful sores. (*Gently rub one hand on the other.*) But they started walking (*walk all ten fingers*) toward the village anyway. As they went, a miracle happened. They looked at their hands again (*look down at your hands*), and the leprosy was gone. The men could hardly believe their eyes. (*Rub your eyes with your hands.*) They were healed! (*Clap your hands together.*)

The Bible says that only one man (*hold up one finger*) came back to say thank you to Jesus. This man fell down on the ground at Jesus's feet, thanking him for what he had done. Jesus asked, "Didn't I heal ten men? (*Hold up all ten fingers.*) Where are the other nine?" (*Put down one thumb.*)

The Bible doesn't tell us why the other nine men didn't come back to thank Jesus. We have to use our imaginations. Maybe the other men were just so excited that they forgot to say thank you. Maybe some of them had some things they wanted to do first. They were too busy. We don't know for sure why only one man said thank you.

But we do know that all the good things in our lives come from God. The Bible (*hold your hands together, palms up, like an open book*) says, "Whatever is good and perfect comes to us from God above" (James 1:17 NLT). Some days we might forget to say thank you to God too. We might just get too busy or too excited when something good happens to say a prayer of thanks. So let's pray right now with our eyes open. Let's use our fingers to tell God ten things we are thankful for. Dear God, thank you for . . . (*Prompt children to call out their responses. Repeat what they say as you count on your fingers to ten. Have several responses ready to add yourself if needed.*) We love you, Lord. Amen.

**Field Experience:** You cannot force children to participate in a children's sermon, but you can encourage them. As you are getting started you can say, "This is going to be fun, so I want everyone to use their hands." If participation starts to fade in the middle of the story, you can encourage them by saying, "Wait, we need to try that again. I didn't see everyone's hands moving."

**Other Children's Sermon Possibilities:** Any Bible story that involves numbers and/or action can be given hand motions. What about telling the creation story by counting out the days on your fingers and creating a hand motion to represent the objects created on each day?

# A New Creation

**Bible Texts:** Acts 9:1–20; 2 Corinthians 5:17

**Message:** God changes us on the inside.

**Preparation:** You will need to create three large posters for this children's sermon: one with a caterpillar on the front and a picture of Saul (an angry-looking biblical man) and his name on the back; one with a cocoon on the front and a bright light with "Met Jesus" on the back; one with a large butterfly on the front and a picture of Paul (a happy-looking biblical man) and his name on the back. You can have someone draw these images for you or find pictures and enlarge them. You will need volunteers or children to help hold these posters while you deliver the message.

**Script:** Did you know that butterflies can teach us about a person in the Bible? It's true. Butterflies teach us about a man named Paul. Let me show you what I mean.

Butterflies are not born as butterflies. They are born as caterpillars. (*Hold up caterpillar poster.*) They creep and crawl on the ground. That's how they start out in life. Then caterpillars find a spot on a leaf or a tree branch to stick to and begin building a covering around them called a cocoon. (*Hold up cocoon poster.*) At just the right moment, the caterpillar breaks out of the cocoon and is a spectacular butterfly. (*Hold up butterfly poster.*) Isn't that an amazing change?

The story of this butterfly reminds me of the story of Paul found in the book of Acts. Paul was not always known as Paul. When he was born his name was Saul. (*Turn the caterpillar poster over to reveal the picture of Saul.*) Saul did not believe that Jesus was the Son of God. He did not follow Jesus. In fact, he tried to stop people from following Jesus. This is what the Bible says: "Saul was going everywhere to devastate the church. He went from house to house, dragging out both men and women to throw them into jail" (Acts 8:3 NLT).

One day, Saul was traveling with two friends to a town named Damascus to arrest the Christians who lived there. As they were walking along, a bright light from heaven suddenly beamed down on Saul. (*Turn over the cocoon poster.*) He fell to the ground. The light was so bright, he couldn't see anything. But he could hear. And what he heard was amazing. He heard Jesus say, "Saul! Saul! Why are you hurting me?" Jesus was telling Saul that by hurting people who followed Jesus, it was like hurting Jesus himself. Suddenly, Saul realized that he had been completely wrong about Jesus.

Saul changed into a new person. (*Turn the butterfly poster around.*) He didn't really change on the outside. The changes in Saul were on the inside. He believed that Jesus was the Son of God. His heart was filled with God's love. He wanted to tell everyone about God's Son, Jesus. God gave Saul a new name to show that he had become a new person. Saul's new name was Paul. Paul even wrote: "Those who become Christians become new persons. They are not the same anymore, for the old life is gone. A new life has begun!" (2 Cor. 5:17 NLT).

The more we know about Jesus, the more we love him; the more we follow him, the more we are changed from the inside out just like Paul was changed. We don't change into butterflies! We change into people who are more and more like Jesus.

Let's pray together. Dear God, change us from the inside out. Make us into people who love you and live for you. In Jesus's name, amen.

**Field Experience:** Be sure the posters are large enough to be seen by the children and most of the congregation. If your sanctuary has screens, project the same images on the screen while you are delivering the children's sermon.

**Take-Home Component:** There are many ways to extend learning beyond the children's sermon time with the topic of butterflies. You could provide a take-home butterfly craft and brief devotional for families. I visited one church that had a hanging caterpillar display in the children's ministry area of the building. Each week, the children checked on the progress of the caterpillars. When the caterpillars changed into butterflies, the children released them outdoors.

## Basket Bible Stories

**Bible Texts:** Exodus 2:1–9; John 6:1–13; Acts 9:23–25

**Message:** God uses ordinary things and ordinary people to do his work.

**Preparation:** You will need lots of baskets: one basket, a baby doll, and a small blanket for the Moses story; one small basket for the boy's lunch and twelve baskets for the leftovers; one large basket a child could climb into for the story of Paul being lowered down the city wall.

**Script:** Today I am going to tell you three Bible stories that all have to do with baskets. I want you to know that God uses ordinary things, like baskets, and ordinary people, like you and me, to do his work. Turn on your ears, your brains, and your hearts and listen to these "Basket Bible Stories."

Our first Bible story is found in the book of Exodus. It is about a little baby boy named Moses. Moses was born at a very dangerous time. His family lived in the country of Egypt. Egypt was ruled by a pharaoh, which is like a king. Pharaoh did not worship God. He did not like people who worshiped God. Moses's parents worshiped God, and they knew that God had very special plans for their little baby boy. They knew that they had to protect baby Moses from Pharaoh. So Moses's mother made a special basket boat for baby Moses. (*Hold up the small basket.*) She gently placed him inside (*place the baby doll in the basket*), wrapped him in a blanket (*add the blanket*), and put the basket boat into the river. She hoped that God would float Moses to a place where he would be safe from Pharaoh. That's exactly what happened. God used that basket boat to float Moses to a safe place where he could grow up and be a great leader for God's people. (*Put the basket to the side.*)

Our second story is found in the book of John. It's about a little boy and his lunch basket. (*Hold up the lunch basket.*) Does your mom ever pack a lunch for you? What does she usually put in your lunch box? The mom in our story packed a lunch of five small loaves of bread and two fish for her little boy. The little boy took his lunch basket and climbed up a mountainside to hear Jesus teach. Lots of other people were there to hear Jesus. After a while, everyone started to get hungry. There were no restaurants around. There were no grocery stores. The only food to be found was in the little boy's basket. He gave this basket to Jesus, and Jesus performed a miracle. Each time he reached into the basket there were more fish and more loaves of bread inside. There was enough food to feed the whole crowd. When everyone was full, the disciples gathered up the leftover food. There were twelve baskets of leftovers. (*Count out the bread baskets with the children.*) Isn't that amazing?

Our third story is found in the book of Acts. It's about a man named Saul. Saul used to hate Jesus. He used to try to hurt people who followed Jesus. But one day, Saul actually met Jesus and it completely changed him. His name was even changed to Paul. From that day on, Paul loved Jesus and told many, many people about him. But some of Paul's old friends did not like how Paul had changed. They did not like him telling people about Jesus. When Paul came to the city of Jerusalem, his old friends planned to capture him and have him killed. Paul heard about their evil plans and asked some of his new friends, friends who loved Jesus, to help him. Paul's new friends got a big basket like this one (*hold up large basket*) and they placed Paul inside. Will someone get inside this basket for me? (*Place the child inside the basket.*) When it was dark, they carried the basket with Paul inside to an opening in the city wall. In those days, the city of Jerusalem was surrounded by a big wall. With ropes, they lowered the basket down the outside of the wall. Paul got away safely and went to many different countries to tell people about Jesus. (*Lift the child out of the basket.*)

So what story does this basket remind us of? (*Hold up the basket from Moses story.*) And how about all these baskets? (*Hold up the baskets from the story of the little boy and his lunch.*) And how about this big basket? (*Hold up the basket from the Paul story.*)

Let's pray together. Dear God, we praise you. You use ordinary things, like baskets, and ordinary people, like us, to do your work. Thank you for these great stories. We love you, Lord. Amen.

**Field Experience:** This children's sermon may take a little more time than usual. Plan to use it on a Sunday when there are not a lot of other things going on in the service. Practice the stories so the details flow smoothly and do not take too much time to relate. If you are still concerned about time, turn this message into a three-part series using one story per week. Be sure to review the basket story (with the baskets) from the previous week to reinforce the Bible stories.

**Other Children's Sermon Possibilities:** These stories share a common object—baskets. The baskets become a clever way to help children remember and relate stories to one another. Think of other Bible stories with a common object that can be linked together: stories with rocks; stories with bread; stories involving water; or stories that take place at night or on a mountaintop.

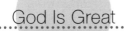

## God Is Great

**Bible Text:** Genesis 11:1–9

**Message:** Our job is to tell everyone that God is great.

**Preparation:** You will need lots of soft building blocks. Prepare three signs—one that says "We are great!" another that says "God is great!" and another that says "I am great!" Put Velcro or double-sided tape on the back of the signs.

**Script:** How many of you like to build things with blocks? Great! I am going to build a big tower with blocks while I tell you a Bible story from the book of Genesis.

Many, many years ago, people on earth spoke the same language. (*Begin to build a tower as you talk. You can invite children to help you. Make the tower big, but do not give it a completed look.*) They could all understand one another. The people gathered together one day and began talking about a construction project. "Here's a great idea," they said. "Let's build a great city with a tower that reaches to the skies. This building and tower will show that we are great." So the people began to build and build and build. The tower got taller and taller and taller. When it was finished, the people were so pleased with themselves. They said, "Look at what we have done. Look at this magnificent tower we have built. We are awesome. We are great." (*Hang the "We are great!" sign on the blocks where the children can see. Read the sign to them.*)

God saw the city and the tower that the people had built. He saw how proud the people were of themselves. It worried God. It seemed that the people had forgotten who was the greatest. Who is the greatest? (*Ask the children.*) God. (*Remove the "We are great!" sign and replace it with the "God is great!" sign.*) God did something very unusual. He gave the people who were building the city and the tower different languages to speak. So when the people went to work on the tower, they couldn't understand each other anymore. The people couldn't work together, so they stopped building the city and the tower and moved on to different places to live and work. The tower was called Babel (which means confusion), and it was never finished.

There may be times when you get a little too proud of yourself. You may get a perfect score on a test. You may score the winning touchdown in a football game. You may be the best reader in your class. You may get the best part in the school play. You may be the person everyone wants to sit by at lunchtime. You may have all the coolest toys at your house. You may start to think, *I am great.* (*Hold up the "I am great!" sign.*) But who is the greatest? God. This story teaches us that God wants us to focus on his greatness and not our greatness. Our job is to tell everyone that God is great. (*Hold up the "God is great!" sign.*)

Let's do that this morning. On the count of three, I want everyone, including adults, to shout, "God is great!" Are you ready? One, two, three . . . God is great!

Let's pray together. Dear God, sometimes we brag about how great we are. We forget that you are the greatest. Help us to tell others about how great you are. We love you. Amen.

**Field Experience:** I recommend soft blocks, foam or cardboard, so that if your tower is knocked over, nobody gets hurt. If you do not have soft blocks, regular building blocks will work.

**Other Children's Sermon Possibilities:** Use soft blocks to tell the story of "Joshua and the Battle of Jericho" or "The Parable of the Two Houses." Children can help knock down the blocks at the appropriate time in the story.

## Joseph and His Brothers

**Bible Texts:** Genesis 37, 39–45; Romans 12:17, 21

**Message:** When people are unkind to us, we are to show them kindness in return.

**Preparation:** This children's sermon involves acting out the story of Joseph with one volunteer playing Joseph and the rest of the children being the brothers. For the action, you will need a "coat of many colors." This can be a colorful bathrobe, a real coat with colorful cloth attached to it, or a large piece of fabric that will be draped over the child. You will also need a large appliance box big enough for a child to fit into. If there is a lot of writing on the outside of the box, you might want to spray paint it black or brown. You will need something to function as chains. I recommend good construction paper links with openings on the end large enough to slip over the child's wrists. Finally, you need something to clothe "Joseph" when he comes to power in Egypt. This may be a sparkly tunic with a modest crown. Use your imagination to come up with something that communicates status.

The child who is playing Joseph will need to go in and out of the appliance box during the children's sermon. You can either lift the child in and out yourself, have a helper do it, or provide a small step stool for the child to climb in and out on his own. Think this through in advance so that you, Joseph, and the "pit" don't come tumbling down in front of the congregation.

**Script:** Today we are telling a story from the Bible about a boy named Joseph. Who wants to be Joseph? (*Pick a boy if possible. If not, a girl will do just fine.*) Joseph, you stand up here with me. Great! Joseph had twelve older brothers. That's a lot, isn't it? Let's pretend that all of you (*point to the rest of the children*) are Joseph's brothers.

Joseph's father loved him in a special way. Joseph was the favorite son. Can you imagine? One day, Joseph's father gave him a beautiful coat of many colors. None of the other brothers got one. This made them very angry at Joseph. Brothers (*to the children*), give Joseph your angriest look. Yikes! To make matters worse, Joseph had several dreams in which his brothers were bowing down to him. Joseph told his brothers about the dreams. They grew even angrier. (*Direct the "brothers" to show an angrier face at Joseph.*)

The brothers decided that they had had enough of Joseph. Tell him (*to the brothers*): "We've had enough of you!"

They found a huge hole in the ground, took off Joseph's coat (*take the coat off Joseph*), and threw him into the hole. (*Get Joseph into the appliance box.*) Right at that moment, a caravan of slave traders was traveling by on their way to Egypt. The brothers decided to sell Joseph to the slave traders so they would never have to see him again. (*Get Joseph out of the hole.*) The brothers were happy that Joseph was gone. Brothers, show me your happy faces.

Joseph, on the other hand, was sad. Joseph, show me your sad face. Now he was a slave. (*Put chains on Joseph's wrists.*) He was put to work in Pharaoh's palace. Pharaoh was the ruler of Egypt. A lot of things happened to Joseph in Pharaoh's palace. He was even thrown into jail for a period of time. But through all the difficulty, Joseph never lost faith in God. He worked hard, and before long, Joseph was given a position of great authority. He was put in charge of the whole land of Egypt. (*Dress Joseph in royal clothes.*)

At the time there was a famine in the land. That means no rain fell to help the crops grow, so there was no food for the people. There was food, however, stored in Pharaoh's palace. Joseph's brothers had no food. Brothers, pretend that you are hungry. They traveled to Pharaoh's palace to try to buy some food. Guess who met them at the front door of the palace? Joseph. Joseph's brothers didn't recognize him. Many years had passed and Joseph had grown up. But Joseph recognized his brothers. His brothers asked him for food. (*Direct the brothers to do this.*) Now he had the chance to get back at his brothers for the ways they had hurt him. What would Joseph do?

Joseph followed God's command. In the Bible we read, "Do not repay anyone evil for evil. . . . Overcome evil with good" (Rom. 12:17, 21). This means do not be mean to someone when they are mean to you. When someone is mean to you, forgive them and treat them with kindness. God forgives us for the things we do wrong, and he wants us to forgive others when they do wrong to us. This is exactly what Joseph did. (*Ask Joseph to go around and shake the hands of his brothers.*) He told his brothers who he was. He forgave them. He gave them all the food they needed. Joseph and his brothers were friends again.

Let's pray together. Dear God, when people are unkind to us, help us to treat them with kindness. Help us to forgive other people just like you forgive us. In Jesus's name, amen.

**Field Experience:** Whenever I do a children's sermon that involves a lot of props, I like to have someone help me carry them out and use them throughout the children's sermon. This extra help frees me up to focus on what needs to be said while my helper focuses on the props.

**Other Children's Sermon Possibilities:** Tell the story of Esther, using different wigs or hats to represent each character—Mordecai, Queen Esther, King Xerxes, and Haman. You can either have a volunteer wear the different wigs or hats or put them on your own head as you tell the story.

## Play Your Part in Noah's Ark

**Bible Text:** Genesis 6–8

**Message:** The Bible is full of exciting stories about God and his people.

**Preparation:** The key to this children's sermon is group participation. Everyone in the sanctuary, including the congregation, has a part to play by saying or doing something on their cue word. Prepare the minister(s) and choir director for their roles in advance. Everyone else can get on-the-spot instructions.

- The choir is **God** in the story. They will sing one "Hallelujah" from Handel's *Messiah*.
- The choir director is **Noah**. He or she will sing one bar of "I'm Singing in the Rain." If you really want to get extra credit for cuteness, you could give Noah an umbrella to hold.
- The minister(s) will help lead the congregation as **the flood**. They will do the wave with their hands. The minister(s) should stand in front of the pews to get the wave started.
- The children are the **animals** on the ark. They need to make animal noises of their choosing at the appropriate time.

It is also a good idea to tape this adapted version of the story into a Bible so that you can "read" it as you go. Be sure to pause after each cue word to give time for participation.

**Script:** I love Bible stories! Today I want you to help me tell one of my very favorite ones. It's the story of Noah's ark found in the book of Genesis. Everyone here, and I do mean *everyone*, has an important part to play. First, we need someone to be God. I have chosen the choir to be God—but don't get too excited; it's just for this story! Every time I say the word *God*, the choir will sing "Hallelujah." Let's practice . . . (*Say "God" and let them sing. Continue this process of assigning parts to the choir director, minister(s), and congregation, having each group rehearse briefly.*)

Finally, all of you (*motion to the children*) are the animals on the ark. I want you to think of an animal that makes a noise and pretend to be that animal—you can be a monkey, a lion, a frog, or whatever you want. When I say the word *animals*, you make your animal noises. Let's practice . . . Great! It sounds like we're ready, so let's tell the story.

Once there was a man named **Noah**. He was a very good man who loved **God** and obeyed all of his commands. Unfortunately, the other people on earth were not so good. They didn't love **God**, and they did whatever they felt like doing. They made the world a miserable place to live. When **God** saw how bad the people were, he was sorry that he had made them. He decided to send a **flood** to destroy the earth and everyone on it, except for **Noah** and his family.

**God** told **Noah** to build a huge boat, called an ark, and to put his whole family on the boat along with two of every kind of **animal**. **Noah** obeyed **God** and built the ark and loaded it with his family and two of every kind of **animal**. When they were all safe inside the ark, **God** shut the door and the **flood** began.

Rain fell on the earth for forty days and forty nights. The waters of the **flood** got higher and higher. The ark began to float. Before long, water covered everything and everyone on earth. But **God** didn't forget about **Noah** and his family and the **animals**.

Finally, the rain stopped. **God** sent a wind to blow across the earth. The waters of the **flood** slowly began to go down. The ark came to rest on a mountaintop. **Noah** sent out a dove several times. When it flew back with an olive branch in its beak, **Noah** knew it was safe to leave the ark. He opened the door of the ark, and his family and all the **animals** walked out onto dry land.

**Noah** and his family gave thanks to **God** for keeping them safe. **God** promised never again to send a **flood** to cover the earth. As a sign of his promise, **God** put the very first rainbow in the sky. And that is the story of **Noah**, the **animals**, and the **flood**.

Let's pray together. Dear God, thank you for Bible stories like this one. Thank you for your promises. Help us to love you and to obey you like Noah. Amen.

**Field Experience:** I have led this children's sermon in two churches of vastly different sizes. It translated well in both settings because it energized the whole sanctuary and created a buzz about telling an otherwise familiar Bible story. I find that choir members typically love to participate in things like this; they are performers by personality. However, you may need to coax the congregation to get into the act. Tell them: "It's for the sake of the children." Do not let them off the hook until they have reached a good energy level with their participation.

If children get carried away with animal noises, say something like, "I'm glad we have so many excited animals in the ark today. But, animals, when I raise my hand, it's time for you to stop making noises and listen to what I say."

**Other Children's Sermon Possibilities:** This technique of assigning different groups parts of a Bible story works well for other familiar stories that have repetitive parts or words. What about "The Fall in the Garden of Eden" (Parts: God, Adam, Eve, snake) or "Daniel and the Lions' Den" (King Darius, king's advisors, Daniel, lions, angel)?

## Playing Hide-and-Seek

**Bible Texts:** Genesis 3; 1 John 1:8–9

**Message:** If we confess our sins to God, he will forgive us.

**Preparation:** None

**Script:** How many of you know how to play the game of hide-and-seek? How would you like to play hide-and-seek this morning in church? Great! I need one person to volunteer to hide. (*Choose a volunteer and tell him or her to hide anywhere in the sanctuary.*) The rest of us, and I do mean all of you (*motioning to the adults*), are going to close our eyes and count out loud to twenty to give our volunteer time to hide. All right, let's get started. Let's close our eyes and count. 1, 2, 3, . . . 18, 19, 20.

I need a few volunteers to go find the person who is hiding. (*Allow several minutes for this to take place. If you need help, ask adults to pitch in with the search. Cheer when the child is found. Then direct the volunteers to rejoin you in the front.*)

Did you know that the first people who lived on earth invented the game of hide-and-seek? Their names were Adam and Eve. Their story is found in the book of Genesis, chapter 3. We played our game of hide-and-seek this morning for fun. But when Adam and Eve played hide-and-seek for the first time, it was because they were in trouble.

You see, God had given Adam and Eve the perfect place to live. It was called the Garden of Eden. In the Garden of Eden, Adam and Eve had everything they needed to be happy. God even visited the Garden of Eden to talk with Adam and Eve face-to-face. It was paradise. God gave Adam and Eve some instructions about life in the Garden of Eden. He told them they could eat anything they found growing there except for the fruit from the tree of the knowledge of good and evil. That tree was off-limits to them. It was the only rule God set for Adam and Eve. And do you know what happened when God wasn't around? They ate the fruit from the tree of the knowledge of good and evil. They both took a bite of the fruit. They broke the one rule God had asked them to follow. They sinned.

Let me read to you what happens next (*read Gen. 3:8–9 from the Bible*): "Then the man and his wife heard the sound of the LORD God as he was walking in the garden in the cool of the day, and they hid from the LORD God among the trees of the garden." Why do you think Adam and Eve hid from God? (*Let the children respond.*) Because they were afraid of getting in trouble. Maybe they were even afraid that God would stop loving them.

When *we* do something wrong, when we break one of God's rules, when we sin, we sometimes act like Adam and Eve. We try to hide it. We pretend that we haven't done anything wrong. If we get caught, we make excuses like "It wasn't my fault," or "Everyone else was doing it." But the Bible teaches us that we should not hide our sin from God. It says we should tell God what we have done wrong. It says: "If we claim to be without sin, we deceive ourselves and the truth is not in us. If we confess our sins [if we tell God what we have done wrong and that we are sorry about it], he . . . will forgive us our sins and purify us from all unrighteousness" (1 John 1:8–9). So don't hide from God; talk to him and tell him what you've done wrong so that you can experience his forgiveness.

Let's pray together. Dear God, sometimes we are like Adam and Eve. We try to hide the things we have done wrong. Instead, help us to pray to you and ask for your forgiveness. In Jesus's name, amen.

**Field Experience:** You might want to pick your volunteers in advance for this sermon. Prepare the child for exactly what you want him or her to do. It can be hard to select someone on the spot when lots of little hands are bobbing up and down. Getting your volunteer lined up in advance will save you time.

**Other Children's Sermon Possibilities:** This children's sermon relies on a familiar game to teach a spiritual truth. "Simon Says" or "Mother, May I" are other games that can be used to teach children about following God's instructions.

## Stop!

**Bible Text:** Luke 19:1–10

**Message:** Jesus will never stop loving us, but he does want us to stop doing what is wrong.

**Preparation:** Each child will need a small stop sign to hold up. You will need one too.

**Script:** Good morning, everyone! Today I am going to need your help telling the story of Zacchaeus found in the book of Luke in the Bible. Will you help me? Great! I am going to pass out these stop signs, one for each of you. (*Make sure every child receives one.*) In our story today, every time you hear the words *stop* or *stopped* or *stopping*, I want you to hold up your stop sign. You must listen very closely. Here we go!

Once there was a man named Zacchaeus. He was a tax collector. It was his job to collect some money from everyone in town to pay for things that everyone needed, like roads and water and policemen. But Zacchaeus kept some of the money for himself. He loved money and the things that money could buy. He just couldn't seem to **stop** taking it from other people. Over time, Zacchaeus became very rich, but he did not have many friends. The people in town knew that Zacchaeus was stealing their money. They **stopped** wanting to be around him.

One day, Zacchaeus heard that Jesus was **stopping** by his town. Zacchaeus had heard that Jesus was God's Son and that he was like no other person who had ever lived. He had heard that Jesus had healed people and worked many miracles. He really wanted to see Jesus for himself. And so did everyone else in town. There was a huge crowd all along the city streets. Zacchaeus couldn't see anything. He was very short. So he decided to climb up into a tree to get a better look at Jesus. Before long, Jesus came right to the bottom of that tree and **stopped**. Jesus looked up into the tree and said . . . well (*to the children*), do you know what Jesus said? (*Let them give the answer . . . or say it yourself.*) He said, "Zacchaeus, come down from that tree. I am going to your house today!"

The people in the crowd couldn't **stop** staring at Jesus and Zacchaeus. Didn't Jesus know that Zacchaeus stole money? Why would Jesus hang out with the worst guy in town?

Zacchaeus couldn't **stop** smiling. He was so excited that Jesus wanted to spend time with him. He scrambled down that tree and led Jesus straight to his house. After Zacchaeus visited with Jesus, he decided that he was going to **stop** taking other people's money. In fact, Zacchaeus gave the money back to the people he had taken it from and used the rest of his money to help poor people. Zacchaeus **stopped** doing what was wrong and started to follow Jesus's rules for his life.

I want you to remember two important things from the story of Zacchaeus. First, Jesus never **stopped** loving Zacchaeus. Even when Zacchaeus was stealing money, Jesus loved him. Jesus loves you too. He loves you when you are doing right and when you are doing wrong. Jesus will never **stop** loving you.

Second, when Zacchaeus got to know Jesus, he **stopped** doing what was wrong. Zacchaeus became different on the inside. Instead of taking money, Zacchaeus gave it to others. Is there anything you are doing wrong that you need to **stop**? Are you disobeying your parents, or saying things that are not true, or being unkind to someone? Jesus wants you to **stop** doing what is wrong.

Would you put your hands together, close your eyes, and say this prayer after me? Dear Jesus, thank you for always loving me. Help me to stop doing what is wrong and do what is right. I love you. Amen.

**Field Experience:** Encourage children to keep holding up their signs by saying, "Let's do that again with everyone participating," or "The girls are doing a good job of participating. Boys, can you do even better?"

**Other Children's Sermon Possibilities:** Repeating words or phrases is a great way to tell stories. How about the story of God calling the boy Samuel, "Samuel, Samuel," or Peter denying Jesus three times, or the creation story—repeat the phrase "It was good."

## The Statue of Gold and the Fiery Furnace

**Bible Text:** Daniel 3

**Message:** We are to obey God's rules even when nobody else is being obedient.

**Preparation:** You will need gold material to wrap around a child to create the golden idol. This can be either shiny gold fabric or wrapping paper. Other necessary supplies are a crown and enough strips of red crepe paper to distribute to all the children. You need music of some sort to cue everyone to bow down to worship the idol. This can be either recorded music that you have someone play through the church sound system or live musicians who create the effect.

**Script:** (*Distribute the strips of red crepe paper as the children come to the front.*) This morning I need all of you to help me tell a Bible story. I have given you a piece of red crepe paper. This will be the fire (*demonstrate how to wiggle it*) in our story. Let me see you make fire (*children participate*). That looks terrific! Now put your fire on the ground and leave it there until I tell you to make fire.

Our story today is found in the book of Daniel. It's about a king named Nebuchadnezzar. Say that with me—Nebuchadnezzar. That's me! (*Put the crown on your head.*) Nebuchadnezzar ruled the kingdom of Babylon. He *did not* worship God. In the kingdom of Babylon, there were three young men with funny names who *did* worship God. Their names were Shadrach, Meshach, and Abednego. Say those names with me—Shadrach, Meshach, Abednego. I need three people to volunteer to be these three young men. (*Select three children and have them stand together in the middle of the other children.*)

One day, King Nebuchadnezzar had an idea. He decided to build a huge statue of gold. I need a volunteer to be the statue. (*Pick the tallest child who volunteers and quickly wrap him or her in the gold material.*) Nebuchadnezzar thought it would be a great idea to have everyone in the kingdom of Babylon gather in front of the golden statue and bow down to worship it. (*To the children:*) I need you all to stand up in front of the golden statue.

(*Make the decree in a royal voice*) "I, King Nebuchadnezzar, order you to bow down and worship this statue of gold when you hear the music play. If you do not bow down and worship this statue, I will throw you into a fiery furnace."

So the music played (*play music*) and all the people in the kingdom of Babylon bowed down and worshiped the golden statue (*demonstrate and then encourage the children to bow down to the ground*) except three young men: Shadrach, Meshach, and Abednego. (*Direct the three children to remain standing.*) They stood tall. They refused to bow down and worship anything. Who did Shadrach, Meshach, and Abednego worship? God! They obeyed God even when nobody else was being obedient.

Well, King Nebuchadnezzar was angry. He ordered the young men to be brought before him, and he said (*in an angry royal voice*), "Is it true that you refuse to worship the statue of gold that I have created? I will give you another chance to obey me. When you hear the music, bow down and worship this statue or I will throw all three of you into a furnace of fire!"

So the music played (*play music*) and all the people in the kingdom of Babylon bowed down and worshiped the golden statue (*encourage the children to bow down to the ground*) except Shadrach, Meshach, and Abednego. They refused to bow down. They worshiped God only. They obeyed God even when nobody else was being obedient.

King Nebuchadnezzar was furious. He fired up the furnace as hot as he could (*direct the children to wiggle their red crepe paper*) and threw Shadrach, Meshach, and Abednego inside.

And then a miracle happened. Shadrach, Meshach, and Abednego were not burned up at all. They were happily walking around in the fire. And then a fourth person appeared in the fire, an angel of God, protecting the three men. The king was amazed. He turned off the fiery furnace (*have the children put their flames back on the ground*), brought Shadrach, Meshach, and Abednego out of the furnace, and ordered everyone in the kingdom of Babylon to worship the one true God. The end!

(*To the children*) Put your hands together and close your eyes, and I'm going to pray for us. Dear God, sometimes we feel pressure from other people to say and do things that are wrong. Give us the courage of Shadrach, Meshach, and Abednego. Help us to obey you even when nobody else is being obedient. In Jesus's name, amen.

**Field Experience:** You can create a golden statue prop instead of wrapping a volunteer in gold material.

**Other Children's Sermon Possibilities:** The other story from the book of Daniel children love is "Daniel in the Lions' Den." Purchase or make lion masks for the children. Secure a costume for Daniel, the king, and an angel, and have fun acting out this story with the children.

## The Story of the Seeds

**Bible Texts:** Mark 4:1–8, 13–20

**Message:** "The Parable of the Sower" teaches us how we grow as Christians.

**Preparation:** For this retelling of "The Parable of the Sower," you will need four children to volunteer to be the seeds. Provide each "seed" with a plain brown baseball cap. You will also need two Bibles, a stuffed animal or hand puppet bird, a cutout of the sun, a small flower or live plant, and a large bouquet of flowers or a large live plant. Finally, write the following eight words or phrases on separate pieces of paper: television, toys, clothes, computer games, sports, after-school activities, homework, playing with friends.

**Script:** Good morning! Jesus told his friends special stories to help them understand God. These stories were called parables. Today I am going to get you to help me retell "The Parable of the Sower," found in the fourth chapter of the book of Mark.

We are calling our story "The Story of the Seeds." I need four volunteers to be the seeds. (*Call up four children who volunteer and give them each a brown baseball cap to wear to make them look more like seeds. Have them sit on the floor until you are ready to tell their portion of the story.*) Here's the story Jesus told . . .

Once upon a time, there was a farmer who was planting seeds. The farmer threw the seed out (*pretend to throw out seeds*) so it would land on the ground and grow.

As the farmer was throwing out the seed, some seed landed on the path (*have one "seed" stand up*). As soon as the seed landed on the path, birds swooped down and ate the seed (*use stuffed animal or puppet to gently peck at the seed as if eating*). Yum! Yum! (*Have child sit down.*)

Another seed (*have another volunteer stand up*) fell on some soil that looked good on the surface, but underneath it was solid rock. That seed quickly sprouted (*hand volunteer the small flower or plant to hold*), but when the sun shone down on the plant (*hold sun prop over the volunteer*), the plant withered and died because it did not have any roots. (*Direct the volunteer to "wither and die."*)

80

Another seed (*have another volunteer stand up*) fell among thorns and grew into a plant (*hand volunteer the small flower or plant to hold*), but the thorns grew too . . . and before long, the thorns choked the life right out of the plant. (*Gently put your arms around the volunteer and squeeze; then have the child sit down.*)

The last seed (*have the final volunteer stand up*) fell on good soil. It came up and grew and grew and grew until it was a big, beautiful plant. (*Hand the volunteer the bouquet of flowers or large plant; clap your hands.*) Hurray! (*Take the prop back and have the child sit down.*)

Now when Jesus finished telling this story, his friends said, "Jesus, that's a really neat story, but what in the world does it mean?" So Jesus explained the meaning of the story to his friends. He said that people are like the seed the farmer throws out onto the ground. (*Have the first seed stand up.*) Some people are like the seed that falls on the path. Do you remember what happened to that seed? (*Birds ate it.*) Some people hear about God and how God wants us to live (*hand the child a Bible*), but the enemy, the devil, comes and fools people into thinking that God isn't real, so they don't believe in him. (*Take the Bible back and have the volunteer sit down.*)

Some people are like the seed that fell on the rocky soil. (*Have the second seed stand up.*) Do you remember what happened to the seed that fell on the rocky soil? (*The sun caused it to wither because it had no roots.*) These people hear about God and how God wants us to live (*hand the child a Bible*), but as soon as something bad happens to them or if they pray for something that God doesn't give them, they get angry and frustrated and they turn away from God. (*Take the Bible back and have the volunteer sit down.*)

Some people are like the seed that fell on the thorny ground. (*Have the third seed stand up.*) Do you remember what happened to this seed? It was choked by the thorns—it didn't have room to grow. These people hear about God and how God wants us to live (*hand the Bible to the child*), but they are also interested in things besides God. (*Hand the signs to the volunteer to hold as you list them.*)

These people like to watch lots of television, buy lots of toys and clothes, and play lots of computer games. They are involved in sports and after-school activities. They have tons of homework and many friends to play with every day. They are busy. They just don't have much time to spend with God, and so they never really have a relationship with him. (*Take the Bible back and have the volunteer sit down.*)

Some people are like the seed that fell on the good soil. (*Have the fourth seed stand up.*) Do you remember what happened to this seed? (*It grew into a beautiful plant.*) These people hear about God and how God wants people to live (*hand a Bible to the child*), and they believe that God is the most important thing in life. They study the Bible and obey what it says. They pray to God—talking to God about anything and everything and listening to what God tells them. They worship God by singing his praise. They use their talents and their money to do things that will help other people know and worship God. In return, God uses these people to do incredible things for him on earth. (*Have the volunteer sit down.*)

Let me ask you an important question: Which seed do you want to be?

Let's pray together. Dear God, we want to be like the seed that is planted in good soil. We want to grow up to be people who love and serve you completely. Will you please help us to do that? We love you, Lord. Amen.

**Field Experience:** With four different seeds standing up two different times, there is a lot of action in this parable. To keep from getting confused about what happens to the seeds, make sure you know this parable inside and out. Speak clearly, succinctly, and with energy.

**Other Children's Sermon Possibilities:**
Develop a "seed series" of children's sermons, using "The Parable of the Mustard Seed" (Matt. 13:31–32) and "The Parable of the Weeds" (Matt. 13:24–30, 36–43).

# 6

## Concept-Driven Children's Sermons

### A Bible Verse for Life

This children's sermon was inspired by my mom. When Mom was a young girl, her Sunday school teacher challenged the class to memorize a Bible verse from the Psalms starting with the first letter of their first name. My mom's first name is Patricia. She chose the verse "Preserve me, O God, for in thee I take refuge" (Ps. 16:1 RSV).

Mom, thank you for sharing your faith and this Bible lesson with me.

**Bible Text:** 2 Timothy 3:16–17

**Message:** The Bible gives us instructions for life.

**Preparation:** Make copies of the "Bible Verse for Life" handout for each child (see pp. 89–90). If your sanctuary has screens, project the Bible verses you are highlighting in the message so children and adults understand about matching the first letter of your name with the first letter of a Bible verse.

**Script:** How many of you have a Bible at your house? How many of you have your very own Bible? Terrific! There are some people who own Bibles but never read them. Some people think the Bible is too hard to understand. Some people think since the Bible was written so long ago, it doesn't have anything to say about life today. But that just isn't so.

The Bible is awesome! It contains everything we need to know about God and Jesus and the Holy Spirit. Here is what the Bible says about itself: "All Scripture is inspired by God and is useful to teach us what is true and to make us realize what is wrong in our lives. It straightens us out and teaches us to do what is right. It is God's way of preparing us in every way, fully equipped for every good thing God wants us to do" (2 Tim. 3:16–17 NLT). The Bible tells us how God wants us to live as his children. God wants us to read the Bible and do what it says.

I know it can be hard for kids to read the whole Bible. It's pretty big for one thing. There are names and places in the Bible that are hard to pronounce. But I would like to challenge you to learn one special verse in the Bible. I want you to choose a Bible verse that will be your very own Bible verse for life. Here's what to do.

I have a list of some good Bible verses for kids (*hold up the handout*). You will choose a verse that starts with the first letter of your first name. For example, my first name is Beth. My name starts with the letter *B*. (*If your worship space has a screen, project the Bible verses as you go.*) My Bible verse for life is: "Be joyful always; pray continually;

give thanks in all circumstances, for this is God's will for you in Christ Jesus" (1 Thess. 5:16–18). Or if your name begins with a *G* like Gracie, then your Bible verse for life would be: "God is our refuge and strength, an ever-present help in trouble" (Ps. 46:1). Or if your name begins with a *W* like Will, your verse for life would be: "With God all things are possible" (Matt. 19:26).

For some of you, the letter that matches the first letter in your name may be part of an important word in the verse. If your name begins with *X* like Xavier, your verse would be: "Don't let anyone look down on you because you are young, but set an eXample for the believers in speech, in life, in love, in faith and in purity" (1 Tim. 4:12).

Once you have chosen your special Bible verse, I want you to work with your parents to understand what that verse means and how you can use it in your life. For example, my verse is: "Be joyful always; pray continually; give thanks in all circumstances." When I am feeling sad or angry or frustrated, I remember that God tells me to be joyful. When I am worried about something, I remember that God tells me to pray about what is on my mind. When I'm feeling grumpy because I am not getting my way, I remember that God tells me to give thanks in good times and in bad times. This Bible verse shapes how I think and how I act every day. I hope your Bible verse will shape your life too.

Let's pray together. Dear God, thank you for the Bible. Thank you for telling us how to live. Help us to learn the words of the Bible and put them to work in our lives. We love you, Lord. Amen.

**Field Experience:** It is a good idea to have a "Bible emphasis" from time to time in children's ministry. I have found it is wrong to assume that parents know which Bibles to get for their children or even if children really need a Bible for themselves. A children's sermon like this provides an opportunity to share information with parents about how children can benefit from early exposure to the Bible. You may also want to give parents a list of age-appropriate Bibles that your church recommends.

**Other Children's Sermon Possibilities:** Since children are mastering the letters throughout their preschool and early elementary years, connecting spiritual lessons to the alphabet is interesting for children. You could create a children's sermon around thinking of an alphabet of things to be thankful for . . . or noticing all the things God has created starting with the letter *A* and ending with *Z*.

Memorize a Bible verse that begins with the first letter of your first name. Work with your parents to understand what the verse means, who said it, and how the verse can help you be a disciple of Jesus Christ.

**A**s the heavens are higher than the earth, so are my ways higher than your ways and my thoughts than your thoughts.  Isaiah 55:9

**B**e joyful always; pray continually; give thanks in all circumstances, for this is God's will for you in Christ Jesus.  1 Thessalonians 5:16–18

**C**all to me and I will answer you and tell you great and unsearchable things you do not know.  Jeremiah 33:3

**D**elight yourself in the LORD and he will give you the desires of your heart.  Psalm 37:4

The **E**arth is the LORD's, and everything in it, the world, and all who live in it.  Psalm 24:1

**F**or God so loved the world that he gave his one and only Son, that whoever believes in him shall not perish but have eternal life.  John 3:16

**G**od is our refuge and strength, an ever-present help in trouble.  Psalm 46:1

**H**ow great is the love the Father has lavished on us, that we should be called children of God!  1 John 3:1

**I** can do everything through him who gives me strength.  Philippians 4:13

**J**esus Christ is the same yesterday and today and forever.  Hebrews 13:8

**K**now that the LORD is God. It is he who made us, and we are his.  Psalm 100:3

**L**ove the Lord your God with all your heart and with all your soul and with all your mind and with all your strength. Mark 12:30

**M**any, O LORD my God, are the wonders you have done. Psalm 40:5

**N**ow you are the body of Christ, and each one of you is a part of it. 1 Corinthians 12:27

**O**bey your parents in the Lord, for this is right. Ephesians 6:1

**P**raise the LORD, O my soul; all my inmost being, praise his holy name. Psalm 103:1

Starting a **Q**uarrel is like breaching a dam; so drop the matter before a dispute breaks out. Proverbs 17:14

In **R**epentance and rest is your salvation, in quietness and trust is your strength. Isaiah 30:15

**S**alvation is found in no one else, for there is no other name under heaven given to men by which we must be saved. Acts 4:12

**T**rust in the LORD with all your heart and lean not on your own understanding. Proverbs 3:5

Give me **U**nderstanding, and I will keep your law and obey it with all my heart. Psalm 119:34

I am the **V**ine; you are the branches. If a man remains in me and I in him, he will bear much fruit. John 15:5

**W**ith God all things are possible. Matthew 19:26

Don't let anyone look down on you because you are young, but set an e**X**ample for the believers in speech, in life, in love, in faith and in purity. 1 Timothy 4:12

**Y**ou will seek me and find me when you seek me with all your heart. Jeremiah 29:13

Never be lacking in **Z**eal, but keep your spiritual fervor, serving the Lord. Romans 12:11

# A Lesson from Copernicus

**Bible Texts:** Psalm 24:1; Isaiah 43:7

**Message:** God is at the center of all of life.

**Preparation:** You will need a globe to represent the earth. School supply stores and some craft stores carry inflatable globes. You will need a sun. This can be an inflatable beach ball (be sure it's yellow) or a playground ball. If possible, the sun should be larger than the earth. You will also need two signs—one that says "Me" and one that says "God." Use a small strip of Velcro to attach each sign to the appropriate prop. It would also be good to show the children a picture of Copernicus. The Internet is a great source for pictures. If your worship space has screens, be sure to project the pictures or any other graphics you find that relate to the children's sermon. You also need space for volunteers to stand and move around one another to illustrate the Copernican theory.

**Script:** We are going to have a science lesson today about the sun and the earth and the rotation of the planets. Many, many years ago, people believed that the earth stood still at the very center of the entire universe. I need someone to be the earth. (*Choose a volunteer to stand up and hold the earth.*)

People thought that the earth and everyone on it was the most important thing in the universe and that everything else, including the sun, revolved around the earth. I need someone to be the sun. (*Choose a volunteer to stand up and hold the sun.*) Okay, sun (*to the volunteer*), I need you to circle around the earth. (*Direct the volunteer to walk in a circle around the earth.*) Good.

One day, a scientist named Nicolaus Copernicus was studying the skies and the horizon. He watched the way the sun came up in the morning and then went down in the evening. He thought about how the seasons change throughout the year. He decided that people had been wrong in thinking that the earth was a fixed planet in the very center of the universe. Copernicus said the earth was not the center of the universe. The sun is at the center. (*Move the sun volunteer to the center.*) The earth does not sit still. The earth rotates on its axis once a day and circles all the way around the sun once a year. (*Have the earth volunteer turn the globe while walking in a circle around the sun.*) This was a huge discovery. It completely changed the way people thought about the world and their place in it.

Copernicus can teach us a lot about living as followers of Jesus Christ. Sometimes we think that we are the most important thing in the world. (*Attach the "Me" sign to the earth and put the earth volunteer back in the middle.*) We think that it is God's job to make us happy. (*Attach the "God" sign to the sun and have the sun volunteer walk around the earth.*) We think God is here to serve us. But this is not what the Bible says. It says, "The earth is the LORD's, and everything in it, the world, and all who live in it" (Ps. 24:1). God is in charge of everything. The world belongs to God. God is at the center of everything. (*Reverse the placement of the volunteers so the sun is in the center and the earth is moving around it.*) The Bible says that our lives belong to God. He makes us who we are. He is the focus of everything we do. We are here for God's glory—to show that he is great; that he is the most important thing; that he is the center of the universe.

Let's pray together. Dear God, sometimes we get confused about how life works. We put ourselves in the center. We forget that you are in charge of everything. Help us to live for your glory. In Jesus's name, amen.

**Field Experience:** This is one of those children's sermons where the props need to work. Make sure your signs will stick to the sun and the globe. Maybe even use older children or adults who have been prepared in advance so things do not get confusing to the children.

**Other Children's Sermon Possibilities:** Check your local Christian bookstore for books of science experiments that relate to biblical truth. These can be adapted to a worship setting with a little creative thought.

## A Servant Attitude

**Bible Texts:** Mark 10:45; Philippians 2:5–7

**Message:** Following the example of Christ, we are to serve other people.

**Preparation:** Gather the following supplies: a crown, an apron, a hand towel, and cleaning gloves.

**Script:** (*Put on the crown.*) Imagine that you are king or queen for the day. Wouldn't it be grand? You would be in charge of everything. You could do anything. People would wait on you hand and foot. You would be all-powerful. You would be the most important person around.

Jesus knew what it meant to be king of the universe, to be in charge of everything. The Bible tells us that Jesus was with God the Father and God the Holy Spirit from the beginning of time. Jesus had all power. Jesus knew everything. Jesus could do anything. Jesus was King of all.

Jesus came to earth to show us God's love. When he was born as a human, he showed his greatness not by ruling over people and demanding to be served (*take off the crown*) but by becoming a servant himself (*put on the apron and gloves, and hold the towel*). The Bible says: "[Jesus] did not come to be served, but to serve" (Mark 10:45). Jesus talked to people who were lonely. He healed people who were sick. He spent time with children and fed hungry crowds of people. He even washed the feet of his disciples, a job that only house servants would have done. Finally, he willingly died on a cross so that we might be forgiven for our sins. Jesus showed us that greatness in God's kingdom is not about wearing a crown and bossing people around. Greatness in God's kingdom is about serving God and other people.

The Bible tells us: "Your attitude should be the same as that of Christ Jesus" (Phil. 2:5). Just as Jesus served other people, we are to serve others as well. We are to think about what other people need, not just what we need. We are to let others go first instead of pushing our way to the front of every line. We are to spend time with people who are lonely and pray for people who are sick. We are to help feed people who are hungry and give to people who are poor. We are to be loving and kind toward our family and friends. We are to look out for each other. When we do these things, we show that we are children of the King (*put on the crown*).

Pray with me. Dear Jesus, thank you for coming to earth. Help me to serve other people just as you did. Amen.

**Field Experience:** To add something extra to this children's sermon, develop a service project children can participate in either individually or as a group. Children love to help out—this message provides the perfect opening to get them activated.

**Other Children's Sermon Possibilities:** Children love to be first in line! Line them up to get a treat. Then reverse the line so that the front of the line is now the back of the line and vice versa. Pass out treats to everyone as you explain the story of James and John wanting to sit in places of honor in heaven (Mark 10:35–45).

## Bugs in the Bible

**Bible Texts:** Exodus 8:16–19; Proverbs 6:6–8; Matthew 3:4–6

**Message:** The Bible is exciting and interesting to read.

**Preparation:** You will need a flyswatter, a small net, and a can of insect repellant spray. In advance, prepare copies of the "Bug Bible Study" to be passed out after the children's sermon (see p. 98). I bought plastic bug rings (can be ordered from novelty or party supply catalogs), rolled up copies of the Bug Bible Study, and stuck them through the rings. The kids loved them!

**Script:** In the summertime, when the temperature outside is hot and the air feels sticky, bugs are everywhere, aren't they? Mosquitoes buzz and bite. Ants creep and crawl around picnic food. Bees buzz around your head, and spiders spin their webs in the trees. I've even seen a roach or two—yuck! You can swat bugs with a flyswatter (*hold up the flyswatter*), try to catch them with a net (*hold up net*), or keep them from biting you with a little bug spray (*hold up the repellant*), but you can't avoid bugs. They are everywhere!

Did you know that the Bible talks about bugs? It may sound crazy, but it's true. There are bugs in the Bible. You know, there are some people who think that reading the Bible is boring. They think that the stories are so old and hard to understand that it's a waste of time to read the Bible.

But that simply is not true. The Bible is the most exciting book you can ever read. There are wild and crazy stories in the Bible about whales, lions, a talking donkey, a fish with money in its mouth, and yes, even stories about bugs.

But don't just take my word for it. I want you to read the Bible for yourself. I am going to give you a "Bug Bible Study" (*hold up one of the sheets*). I want you to take it home and get your mom or dad or your grandparents to help you look up three stories in the Bible about bugs. And remember: the Bible is exciting and interesting to read because it is God's story for us, bugs and all!

Let's pray. Dear God, thank you for the Bible and all the great stories in it. In Jesus's name, amen.

**Field Experience:** One function of the children's sermon is to equip parents to spiritually train their children at home. Parents are ultimately responsible for passing their faith on to their children. Just bringing them to church is not enough. I look for ways like the Bug Bible Study to make the children's sermon spill over into a homework assignment for parents that is manageable and interesting. In this way, parents can weave church lessons into everyday life with their children.

**Other Children's Sermon Possibilities:** Children love stories that are wild and wacky. You might even plan a series of children's sermons—"Wild and Wacky Bible Stories"—that captures the broad spectrum of stories in the Bible. Stories could include "Balaam's Donkey" (Num. 22:21–39); "Valley of Dry Bones" (Ezek. 37:1–14); and "The Writing on the Wall" (Daniel 5).

## Bug Bible Study

Did you know that the Bible talks about bugs? Read these Scripture passages and answer these questions with your parents. You'll be crawling with excitement about all the cool stuff you can find in the Bible.

- Exodus 8:16–19: How did God use gnats to show his power?

- Proverbs 6:6–8: What can you learn from an ant?

- Matthew 3:4–6: Why do you think John the Baptist ate locusts?

# Double Trouble

**Bible Text:** Psalm 34:12–13

**Message:** Telling the truth is the best way to stay out of trouble.

**Preparation:** You need to prepare a sign that can fold in half. One half of the sign should have the word *Trouble* written on it. When the sign is opened up completely, the second half should also say "Trouble."

**Script:** Is it okay to tell lies? No way! We all know it is wrong to lie. It's one of God's Ten Commandments. But sometimes it is hard to tell the truth. Can you think of a reason why a boy or a girl might feel like telling a lie? (*If nobody suggests it, say, "We often tell lies to keep from getting in trouble when we've done something wrong."*)

Sometimes we may think that lying will keep us out of trouble. What if nobody finds out what we did wrong? Right? But I want to show you today that lying actually gets us into even more trouble.

Imagine your mom has told you not to throw balls inside the house because you might break something. You know this is the rule. But when your mom is outside working in the yard, you and your buddy decide to play a quick game of catch with your new Nerf football. You are having a great time, making some terrific catches, when suddenly your throw sails over your friend's head and hits a fancy plate that your mom has hanging on the wall. It breaks into many pieces. The plate was something special your mom got from her great-grandmother on the day she was married. You know your mom will be furious and you'll be punished for breaking the rule about throwing balls inside the house. At this point, you are in trouble. (*Hold up the "Trouble" sign.*)

You hate getting in trouble. It will probably mean your mom will take your new football away or make you stay at home the next day with no friends; maybe you'll even have to do extra chores around the house to pay for the plate. So you come up with a plan. Maybe if you hide the broken plate at the bottom of the trash can, your mom won't notice the plate is missing. She's very busy anyway. And if she does notice, you can just tell her you have no idea what happened to it. Or, you can blame it on your friend. So that's what you do; you hide the pieces of the plate in the bottom of the trash can and wait.

That night at dinner, your mom says, "What happened to my special plate that was hanging on the wall?" Gulp! She's busy, but she's smart too. You try saying, "I don't know." She doesn't fall for it. Now you try, "My buddy must have broken it when he was throwing my new Nerf football in the house. He doesn't have very good aim." Your mom starts to give you "the look"—the one that tells you she knows that you are not telling her the whole story. At this point, you are in double trouble. (*Flip the hidden part of the sign out so that both "Trouble" signs are showing.*) You are in trouble for breaking the plate, and you are in trouble for telling a lie about it. You will get double punishment. Do you see how that works? It would have been better to tell the truth from the beginning and face *some* trouble than to tell a lie and get *double* trouble.

Now maybe there are some of you who are thinking to yourselves, *What if the lie works? What if I really don't get into any trouble at all? What if my parents never find out what I have done wrong?* Let me tell you clearly, you are still in trouble. Lying is a sin. And when we sin and we are not sorry for it, there is one person who always knows: God! Sin gets in the way of our relationship with God. It is harder for us to pray. It is harder for us to understand the

Bible. It is harder for us to feel close to God. This is what the Bible says in Psalm 34:12–13: "Whoever of you loves life and desires to see many good days, keep your tongue from evil and your lips from speaking lies."

Let's pray and ask God to help us tell the truth even when we know it means getting into some trouble. Dear God, we know that lying is a sin. Sometimes we are afraid to tell the truth. Give us strength to be honest. Help us not to lie. In Jesus's name, amen.

**Field Experience:** At the beginning of this children's sermon, a question is asked of the children. Asking questions can be tricky. You never know what children are going to say. Be sure you have an answer to your own question in case the children do not give you an answer that contributes to the direction of the children's sermon.

**Other Children's Sermon Possibilities:** James 3:2 (NLT) says: "We all make many mistakes, but those who control their tongues can also control themselves in every other way." Tongue control is a great topic for a series of children's sermons. Just like adults, children struggle in the areas of gossip, profanity, rudeness, inappropriate humor, and misusing God's name. Teaching them biblical truth in relationship to these issues will equip them to know why what they say matters to God.

**Bible Text:** Psalm 119:11

**Message:** Memorizing Bible verses helps us take God's Word with us wherever we go.

**Preparation:** Write the words to the following Bible verse on large pieces of paper or poster board. Put one word on each piece of paper, including "Psalm 119:11" on one:

> I have hidden your word in my heart.
>
> Psalm 119:11

If possible, create a simple sketch to illustrate the main words under the text, such as an eye for "I," a picture of the Bible for "word," and a heart symbol for "heart." This will help nonreaders learn the Bible verse. Also, make a handout with this verse and the sketches on it to give to the children. Add two other verses that the children can work on with their parents at home.

**Script:** Good morning, everyone! I brought my Bible with me this morning. How many of you have a Bible at your house? Great! How many of you read the Bible? That's terrific! You and I know that the Bible contains the things God wants us to know about him. The Bible tells us how to live every day.

But it isn't always possible to take your Bible with you wherever you go. If you are going to the swimming pool or the beach, the pages could get wet. If you take the Bible with you to the movies, it's too dark to read it. If you are riding your bike to your friend's house, your Bible might not fit in your back pocket. If you are racing around getting ready for school, you just might forget your Bible because you are in a hurry.

The great thing about the Bible is that you do not have to be carrying one around all the time to know what it says. Psalm 119:11 says, "I have hidden your word in my heart." We can hide the words of the Bible in our hearts. That means we can memorize Bible verses so we can say them without reading them from the Bible, just like we memorize our phone numbers so we can call home without having to look in a phone book.

I am going to teach you a fun and easy way to learn a Bible verse from memory. I need nine adult volunteers to stand up in front with me. (*Select the volunteers and hand each one a poster. Make sure the posters are in the right order when you hand them out.*) This is the verse from the Bible I just read. I will read it again: "I have hidden your word in my heart." Psalm 119:11. (*Point to each word as you read it slowly. If you have sketches on your posters, you may want to explain how they relate to the words of the verse.*) This last part says "Psalm 119:11"; that is where this verse is found in the Bible. It is kind of like the address for the Bible verse—it tells you exactly where it is found. "Psalm" is the book of the Bible, "119" is the number that tells the chapter, and "11" is the number that tells the verse.

Now I want you to read this verse with me. (*Repeat the verse slowly.*) Next, we are going to remove one of the words and see if you can still say the whole verse. (*Have the volunteer holding "hidden" turn the poster around so the children cannot see it. Say the verse along with the children, pointing to the blank poster and letting them fill in the word.*) That was great! Do you think you can still say the Bible verse if we remove another word? Let's try it. (*Remove "heart."*) Good job! Let's keep going. (*Remove the words one by one until the children can say the Bible verse from memory.*)

That's excellent! I hope you will keep working on this verse and several others that I have for you today. I'll give you this handout (*hold it up*) after we pray. It has three verses on it—the one we just memorized and two others. You can cut the verses apart into separate cards and play your own memory game at home with your parents.

Let's pray together. Dear God, thank you for the Bible. Help me to hide your words in my heart so I can love you and serve you wherever I go. I love you, God. Amen.

**Field Experience:** I have used this memory game to teach children as young as three a Bible verse. The children love the sense of accomplishment they feel from learning a Bible verse so quickly. You may want to include the adults in this children's sermon by asking them to participate along with the children in saying the verse aloud.

**Other Children's Sermon Possibilities:** Using sign language to teach Bible verses is another great technique for children's sermons. *Sign & Say Bible Verses for Children* and *More Sign & Say Bible Verses for Children* (Robert S. Jones, illustrator; Daphna Flegal, editor) are great resources for age-appropriate verses and sign language.

## How Fast Are You?

**Bible Text:** Psalm 119:60

**Message:** God wants us to obey quickly.

**Preparation:** You will need a stopwatch.

**Script:** Good morning, everyone. Do you like to run fast? Today, I need one of you to run as fast as you can all the way around the sanctuary. I am going to time you with this stopwatch to see how fast you can run. Who wants to give it a try? (*Select a volunteer. If you don't already know the child's name, find it out now.*)

Okay, everyone, we need to clear a path for (*child's name*) to make it around the sanctuary. Not on the outside of the sanctuary but on the inside, around the seats! All you grown-ups out there need to keep your hands and feet and purses out of the aisles. (*To the child:*) Take a few deep breaths. On your mark, get set, go! (*When the child returns to the front, announce the time.*) Wow, you are really fast. Thanks for running for us.

Did you know that the Bible tells us we should be fast about doing something else besides running? Psalm 119:60 says, "I will hasten and not delay to obey your commands." The word *hasten* means to be in a hurry, to be fast. So let me read the verse again, and you tell me what we are supposed to do quickly. "I will hasten [or hurry, or be fast] and not delay to obey your commands." What must we do in a hurry? Obey.

God must have put this verse in the Bible because he knows that we are often s-l-o-w (*say it slowly for greater emphasis*) to obey his commands. Our parents ask us to come to the dinner table, and we say: "Not yet . . . in a minute . . . after I finish this computer game." Jesus tells us to share what we have with those who are in need, and we say: "I haven't had a turn yet; wait until I'm finished." We know it is important to read the Bible and to pray every day, but we say: "I'll do that later; I don't feel like it right now." This verse teaches us it is important to God that we obey quickly.

Let's ask God to help us do that. Dear God, we admit that we often obey you slowly. We make excuses, we stall, we try things our way first, we dillydally. Forgive us, Lord. Help us to be fast to obey your commands. Amen.

**Field Experience:** Depending on your time constraints, you can have more than one child run around the sanctuary. It is also fun to have the congregation cheer for the runner. If running in church goes against your grain, consider this quote from Brant Baker, author of *Let the Children Come*: "Running, crawling, skipping, and wiggling not only epitomize learning by doing, but help overcome stereotypes of church as a stiff and somber place. There must be respect in worship, but there should be joy!"[1]

**Other Children's Sermon Possibilities:** Obedience is a major issue in childhood—and adulthood, for that matter. Other pertinent Bible verses about the quality of our obedience that would make great children's sermons include:

- Ephesians 6:1—Obedience to parents is related to obeying God.
- Philippians 2:14—We should obey without complaint or argument.
- John 14:23—Obedience is a tangible way to show our love for God.

**Bible Text:** Revelation 21:3–4

**Message:** Life in heaven will be perfect.

**Preparation:** Place the following items in a bag or box: a bandage, a tissue, a night-light, and a question mark (cut the shape from a piece of construction paper).

**Script:** I have some exciting news for you today. If you believe in Jesus, you have *two* lives to live. You have *one* life to live here on earth. And when you die, you will have *another* life to live in heaven that will go on forever and ever. Two lives—isn't that cool?

Now some of you may be wondering, *What will life be like in heaven?* To find the answer to this question, we need to look in the Bible. One of Jesus's disciples, John, saw a picture of heaven and wrote about it in the book of Revelation—the very last book in the Bible. I have brought some things with me to show you what the disciple John said about heaven.

First, I have a bandage. (*Pull the bandage out of the bag.*) We need bandages and medicine on earth. We get scrapes and scratches and bruises. But not in heaven! We won't get hurt. We won't get sick. There will be no pain in heaven. Our heavenly bodies will work perfectly all the time.

Next, I have a tissue. (*Pull the tissue out of the bag.*) We need these on earth. Sometimes we cry when things happen that make us sad or people hurt our feelings. We may get in trouble for the things we do wrong; that makes us cry. Maybe our pets die or our best friend moves to another town. Those things make us cry too! But there will be no

107

crying in heaven. We won't need tissues in heaven because there will be no sadness or sin or death.

I also have a night-light. (*Pull the night-light out of the bag.*) There are dark places on earth. Sometimes the darkness is scary to us even in our own bedrooms. So on earth, we use night-lights to help us not be afraid of the dark. But we won't need night-lights in heaven because there will be no darkness there. In fact, the Bible says that in heaven, God will be our light. We won't need lightbulbs at all.

The best thing about heaven is that God will be there. The Bible says that we will see God's face. He will live with us and visit with us in person. That means you will have the chance to ask God all the questions you might have about life on earth. That's why I have a question mark with me. (*Pull the question mark out of the bag.*) On earth, we have a lot of questions that nobody can answer, not even our parents. In heaven, God will give us the answers to all of our questions—big ones like, "Why did my grandmother die?" and little ones like, "Why did you make ants?"

No pain, no crying, no darkness, no more questions that have no answers, and seeing God in person—doesn't life in heaven sound awesome?

Put your hands together and close your eyes and repeat this prayer after me: Dear God, thank you for heaven. It sounds like a wonderful place to live. We are excited about living there with you one day. We love you. Amen.

**Field Experience:** You may want to give the children their own bag with supplies in it. They can find the items in their bag as you pull out the items from your bag. Or they can use the supplies in their bags to tell someone else what heaven will be like.

**Other Children's Sermon Possibilities:** Children have lots of questions about heaven. Ask them to write down their questions and send them to you. Compile the list and answer as many questions about heaven as you can during a children's sermon. Publish the list of the children's questions in your church bulletin or newsletter.

## The One Thing Jesus Cannot Do

**Bible Text:** 2 Corinthians 5:21

**Message:** Jesus is the only perfect person who has ever lived.

**Preparation:** None

**Script:** Jesus is amazing, don't you think? Jesus existed before time. He was with God when the whole world was created. And then, at a certain time, he came to earth. He was born as a baby. He lived on earth just like you and me. Jesus was a person. But at the same time, Jesus was still God. That means he could do things no other person could do. Jesus had the power to do some amazing things. Listen to all the unbelievable things Jesus did while he was on earth:

- Turned water into wine
- Walked on water
- Stopped a storm
- Fed 5,000 people with a young boy's lunch
- Made a blind man see
- Helped a lame man walk

- Cured a boy of evil spirits
- Healed a girl who died
- Raised his friend Lazarus back to life
- Healed a soldier's ear that had been cut off
- Forgave people's sins
- Died on the cross and came back to life again

Isn't that a list of awesome things? Jesus can do anything . . . (*hesitate for a few seconds*) well, almost anything. When I think about it, there is one thing that Jesus cannot do no matter what. Jesus cannot do anything wrong. He just can't. Jesus cannot break any of God's rules. Jesus cannot sin. Jesus is perfect in every way. In fact, Jesus is the only perfect person who has ever lived on earth.

That is why Jesus is able to save us from our sins. Only Jesus could die for our sins because he was the only person who had never done anything wrong. He exchanged his perfect life for our messed-up lives so that when God thinks about us, he doesn't think about our sin; he thinks about Jesus's perfection.

I don't know about you, but when I think about Jesus and the perfect life he lived, it makes me want to fall on my knees and worship him. Let's do that right now. Will you get on your knees with me? Now put your hands together and close your eyes and repeat this prayer after me: Dear Jesus, we worship you. You are perfect in every way. You are amazing. Thank you for giving your perfect life to save us from our sins. We love you. Amen.

**Field Experience:** This is a children's sermon where children mainly sit and listen, except for when they get on their knees to pray. Therefore, your enthusiastic tone of voice is important to maintain the children's attention.

**Other Children's Sermon Possibilities:** How about "Who Is the World's Greatest Superhero?" Compare Jesus to the other superheroes children love. Talk about how Jesus can do things for us that no other superhero can do.

## The Right Time to Pray

**Bible Text:** 1 Thessalonians 5:17

**Message:** We can pray at any time of the day.

**Preparation:** You will need a large clock with hands you can easily move.

**Script:** I am going to ask you some questions about what time of day you do certain things. (*Hold up the clock. As children call out their responses, move the hands of the clock to the appropriate time.*)

- What time do you get up?
- What time do you go to school?
- What time do you eat lunch?
- What time do you do your homework?
- What time do you eat dinner?
- What time do you go to bed?

There are certain times of day when we do certain things.

111

Let me ask you an important question: What time do you pray? (*Listen to responses from children.*) You might pray in the morning when you wake up or at night before you go to bed. You probably pray before you eat each meal of the day.

The Bible teaches us that there is a right time of day to pray. Do you know what time that is? All the time! (*Move the hands of the clock completely around.*) The Bible says in 1 Thessalonians 5:17, "Pray continually." Say that with me: "Pray continually." What does *continually* mean? All the time. Without stopping. You see, God wants to be a part of your life moment by moment. He wants you to tell him everything you are thinking and feeling. He is interested in the details of your life.

That doesn't mean you should walk around all day with your hands folded and your eyes closed, talking out loud to God. First of all, you would bump into things and hurt yourself. Second, people might think you're crazy. When you're playing with friends or doing work at school, you can pray from your heart without saying anything out loud at all. You can say quick prayers like:

- "Thank you, God, for this beautiful day."
- "Help me, God, to do well on this test."
- "I'm sorry, God. I just messed up by using bad words."
- "I don't know what to do, God. Will you show me what is right?"

And then, whenever you find some quiet time in your day, it is also a great idea to sit down and fold your hands and close your eyes and talk out loud to God. Will you do that with me right now? Dear God, thank you for always being ready to listen to our prayers. Help us to pray all the time. In Jesus's name, amen.

**Field Experience:** For a fun take-home idea, pass out play watches (found at party supply stores) with the Bible verse attached to remind children to pray all the time.

**Take-Home Component:** A great prayer technique to teach children is "the breath prayer." Instead of saying words out loud, you pray a simple prayer to yourself as you breathe in ("God is with me") and breathe out ("I am not afraid"). Breath prayers are great for children to use at school or on the sports field.

# 7

# Prop-Driven Children's Sermons

## A Friend Loves in All Kinds of Weather

**Bible Text:** Proverbs 17:17

**Message:** True friends stay together in good times and in bad times.

**Preparation:** You will need to prepare two poster cutouts. One should be in the shape of the sun. The other should look like a dark cloud with rain coming out of it.

**Script:** Good morning! If the weatherman says it's going to look like this (*hold up the sun poster*), what kind of day can you expect? A great day, right? If the weatherman says it's going to look like this (*hold up the cloud poster*), what kind of day can you expect? A cloudy, yucky day.

Have you ever heard the phrase "a fair-weather friend"? A fair-weather friend is a friend who sticks with you on good days (*hold up sun poster*). A fair-weather friend is someone who likes to be your friend when things are going well. A fair-weather friend is a friend who is with you when you're having fun, when you've got lots of neat toys, when you're doing fun things and laughing and getting along great. The problem with a fair-weather friend is that when things are not going so well (*hold up cloud poster*), that friend disappears. When things get boring, or your toys are worn-out or broken, or if you're feeling sad, or if there's a fight, fair-weather friends say, "I don't want to be your friend anymore."

The Bible tells us that real friends love in all kinds of weather. (*Hold up both posters.*) Proverbs 17:17 says, "A friend loves at all times." Say that out loud with me. "A friend loves at all times." God wants you to be a friend who loves when things are good, like sunny days, and when things are bad, like cloudy days. God wants you to stay with your friends in happy times and in sad times, when life is fun and when life is boring. When you have a fight with a friend and you're both angry, God wants you to work it out, to forgive each other. A true friend is a friend all the time.

Let's pray and ask God to help us be friends who love one another all the time. Dear God, sometimes it is hard to get along with friends. Help us to be friends in good times and in bad times. Show us how to love and forgive one another. In Jesus's name, amen.

**Field Experience:** Getting along with friends is an important issue for children. Friendships can bring joy and tears to children as they gain skills in getting along with one another. Teaching children how to navigate friendships with biblical principles is something they are very interested in.

**Other Children's Sermon Possibilities:** Here are some possible topics for children's sermons based on friendships:

- Ecclesiastes 4:9–12—Friends help each other.
- Hebrews 10:24–25—Friends encourage each other to do what is right.
- John 15:14–15—Being friends with Jesus.

# Earthly Tents and Heavenly Homes

**Bible Text:** 2 Corinthians 5:1

**Message:** In heaven you will get a new body that lasts forever.

**Preparation:** You will need a pop-up tent. Begin with it folded down and pop it open at the right time.

**Script:** How many of you have camped out in a tent? Great! I brought a tent with me this morning. Let me get it set up. (*Open the tent.*) Tents are really fun to sleep in for a couple of nights, aren't they? But would you like to sleep in a tent forever? What about when it gets really cold outside, or rainy, or windy? Tents are fun to sleep in once in a while, but they do not hold up very well if the weather is not good.

They are made out of fabric that can rip and get damaged. They are temporary; they don't last forever.

We sleep in our houses most of the time. Houses or apartments or condos are made out of concrete, brick, and wood. They protect us better from rain and cold air and wind. Houses are more permanent. They last longer than tents.

Did you know that the body you are living in right now is like a tent? God gave you this body to live in while you are on earth. But your body is like a tent. It doesn't last forever. It gets hurt and sick. One day, your body will just give out.

When you get to heaven, you will get a new body. Your heavenly body will be more like a house. It will be strong and sturdy. It will never get a scrape or cut. It will never get sick. It will never give out. You will live in your heavenly body forever.

The next time you fall down and get a cut or have to go to the doctor because you are sick, I want you to think about heaven and the new body you will have when you get there. Though sometimes it is hard to live in our earthly tents, we know that our heavenly homes will be perfectly wonderful.

Let's pray together. Dear God, thank you for heaven and the new bodies you will give us there. Thank you for loving us so much. We love you, Lord. Amen.

**Field Experience:** I would advise against having children go inside the tent for the children's sermon. If everyone cannot fit in or doesn't get a turn to go inside, it can breed chaos. You can also lose the children's attention if they are more captivated by being in the tent than listening to you. Instead, assure children that the tent will be set up in some central location after church. The children can crawl in and out at that point instead of during the service.

**Other Children's Sermon Possibilities:** Study the Old Testament story of the tabernacle beginning in Exodus 25. The tabernacle was a tentlike structure where God would dwell with the people of Israel while they were traveling through the desert to the Promised Land. There were many regulations about the tent and who could go inside to meet with God. We are New Testament Christians, and God dwells in our hearts through the Holy Spirit. We do not have to go to any special place, not even church, to meet with God. God is with us all the time. We can talk and listen to God anytime, anywhere. Use a pop-up tent to teach this story.

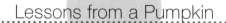

## Lessons from a Pumpkin

**Bible Text:** Acts 17:28

**Message:** God the Father made us. God the Son cleans the sin out of our lives. God the Spirit lives inside of us.

**Preparation:** You will need a good-sized pumpkin. In advance, cut into the pumpkin and scrape out the pulp. Put the pulp onto a small plate or bowl that can fit back inside the pumpkin before the children's sermon. Carve one side of the pumpkin to be a friendly jack-o'-lantern. You will also need a candle and a match. As you begin the children's sermon, turn the carved side away from the children.

**Script:** This time of year we see lots and lots of pumpkins. I brought this pumpkin with me to church today because pumpkins can teach us a lot about God. Let me ask you a question. Who made this pumpkin? God the Father made this pumpkin. He is the creator of all things. God decided that pumpkins should come in all different shapes and sizes. Just as God the Father created this pumpkin, God created you and me. He made people in all different shapes and sizes and colors—so that no two people would be exactly alike.

If you look inside a pumpkin you'll find that it is pretty yucky in there. (*Open the pumpkin and hold up some of the pulp.*) A pumpkin is filled with a lot of goo! You have to clean all that slimy stuff out of the pumpkin. There is something about us that needs to be cleaned up too. It is our sin. Sins are the things we do that break God's rules. Jesus died on the cross to remove the power of sin in our lives. (*Remove the guts of the pumpkin.*) Just as we clean out this pumpkin, Jesus cleans the sin out of hearts and makes us right with God.

But that's not all. God the Spirit comes to live in our hearts. (*Put a candle inside the pumpkin and light it.*) With God's Spirit inside of us, just like this candle inside the pumpkin, it shines out of us in how we act and how we talk and how we treat other people. God's Spirit helps us to shine the love of God into the whole world. (*Turn the pumpkin around so the children can see the smiling jack-o'-lantern.*)

Let's pray together. Dear God, thank you for pumpkins and the things they teach us about you. Thank you for making us. Thank you for sending Jesus to cleanse us of our sins. Thank you for your Spirit who lives inside of us. We love you, Lord. Amen.

**Field Experience:** You will want to practice this children's sermon first. Be sure you can easily remove the guts from the pumpkin. Be sure you can light the candle inside the pumpkin without setting yourself on fire. If you want to be very creative, you can carve a heart out of the front of the pumpkin . . . or a word, such as *God* or *love*.

**Other Children's Sermon Possibilities:** Children love getting ready for Halloween. Dressing up in costumes is fun for them. Perhaps you could have a Sunday when they come to church in costumes—nothing scary, though. Choose several volunteers to show off their costumes. Talk about how they may look one way on the outside, but underneath, they are all children of God. Relate this to 1 Samuel 16:7: "Man looks at the outward appearance, but the LORD looks at the heart."

## God Is Our Fortress

**Bible Text:** Psalm 31:1–3

**Message:** We can talk to God when we are afraid, lonely, or worried.

**Preparation:** Use several large appliance boxes to create a movable fortress. Use spray paint to make it look more authentic. If you have a small group of children, you can pull the walls of the fortress all the way around them. If you have a large group, you may want to create a wall that will wrap around the children but doesn't completely enclose them.

**Script:** Good morning, everybody! I am glad you are here today. How many of you have a tree house or fort that you like to play in? (*Listen to the responses of the children.*) That's great! Did you know that the Bible says God is our fortress? Say that with me . . . God is our fortress.

A fortress is a building that protects people. It has high, thick walls made out of strong, sturdy bricks. I brought a pretend fortress with me this morning. So let's all get inside. (*Set up the fortress and make sure that all the children are behind its walls.*)

God protects us like a fortress. That means when we are afraid, we can talk to God about it and trust him to keep us safe. When we are lonely, we can talk to God about it and trust him to be with us all the time. When we are worried, we can talk to God and trust him to give us exactly what we need. We can pray these words from the Bible straight to God: "Rescue me. . . . Be for me a great rock of safety, a fortress" (Ps. 31:1–2 NLT).

The next time you are afraid, lonely, or worried, I want you to imagine yourself running into God's fortress, telling him how you feel, and asking him to protect you. When you do this, God will help you to feel strong and brave and safe.

Let's pray together. Dear God, you are our fortress. You protect us from all danger. Thank you for keeping us safe. We love you, Lord. Amen.

**Field Experience:** Have several helpers stationed inside the fortress walls to hold them up if necessary and to keep the kids under control. Once you have finished praying, get the volunteer to stand up and remove the fortress walls quickly so none of the children get hurt.

**Other Children's Sermon Possibilities:** Large appliance boxes are great for creating all kinds of props because they are inexpensive and easy to move. Use boxes to make two houses to teach "The Parable of the Wise and Foolish

Builders." Cut out the shape of a boat and the shape of a whale to tell the story of "Jonah and the Whale."

## The Living Cross

**Bible Text:** John 11:25–26

**Message:** The cross is a symbol of life.

**Preparation:** Two simple crosses are used in this children's sermon. One cross should be rough, brown wood. You can add nails and a crown of thorns. This cross will symbolize death. The other cross will symbolize life; it should be covered with floral foam and greenery. The children will insert colorful flowers into the cross during the message. A florist is a great resource for pulling these props together. Be sure the stems of the flowers are trimmed to approximately two inches in length to make it easy for the children to insert them into the floral foam. Have several volunteers on hand to help distribute the flowers and assist the children.

If you have a large number of children, you may wish to insert the flowers in advance. Use a small throw or cloth to cover the crosses until the proper time during your message.

**Script:** Good morning! By looking at all of you, I can tell today is Easter Sunday. I see that lots of you are wearing bright clothes. Have some of you hunted for eggs and filled your Easter baskets? I can guess by the big smiles on your faces that you have.

Eggs and baskets are fun, but here is something else that makes me think of Easter. It is the cross. (*Uncover the brown cross.*) Many, many years ago, people who had done really terrible things were punished by being nailed to a cross to die. So when people saw a cross like this one, they would think of punishment and death.

But then Jesus came to live on earth. Did Jesus ever do anything wrong? No. He lived a perfect life. Because he loved us so much, Jesus was nailed to a cross and died as punishment for the things *we* do wrong. But Jesus did not stay dead. He came back to life. That's what the word *resurrection* means—to come back to life.

What's even more exciting is that Jesus said in the Bible, "If you believe in me, even though you will die, you will also come back to life again." That means Jesus died on the cross, and one day our bodies will give out and we will die too. But just as Jesus came back to life, we will come back to life too . . . and live forever in heaven. So when we see a cross, we think of more than punishment and death. When we see a cross, we think of life.

(*Uncover the cross decorated with greenery.*) To show that we believe Jesus came back to life, I want you to help me bring this cross to life by covering it with beautiful flowers. (*Have the volunteers distribute the flowers to the children and invite them forward to place their flowers in the cross.*)

You did a great job of making this living cross. Let's end our time together by praying to God. Dear God, thank you for Jesus. Thank you for the cross. Thank you for the promise that when we believe in Jesus, we will live with you in heaven forever. We love you, God. Amen.

**Field Experience:** Some children may be shy about participating in this children's sermon. Give children a flower and encourage them. If they are reluctant, assure them quietly, "You can just hold your flower."

124

**Other Children's Sermon Possibilities:** I used this "living cross" concept in a children's sermon at a baby's funeral. The family had elementary children who attended the school at our church. Many of their friends and classmates had been praying for the birth of their baby brother. When little Jacob was stillborn, it was devastating to the family and many of the children at the school. The family wanted the funeral to include a time for the children to express their grief and hear a message of hope. When the children arrived with their parents at the funeral, they were given flowers. I called the children forward for the children's message and they put their flowers in the cross. I talked to them about how sad we all felt and how difficult it was to understand what had happened to baby Jacob and his family. Then I talked to them about the hope we have in Christ, using the passage from 1 Thessalonians 4:13–14 about grieving with hope in the resurrection.

While you may not be faced with preparing a children's sermon for a funeral, I do think this message is an important one for us to communicate with children. Death is a part of life they will experience in one way or another. Knowing how to think about death in light of our faith is critical.

## The Potter and the Play-Dough

**Bible Text:** Isaiah 29:16; 64:8

**Message:** God is shaping you into what he wants you to be.

**Preparation:** Each child will need a small ball of play-dough. You can buy it or make it using the recipe below. I would advise using one color; it will be easier to distribute the play-dough if the children are not making special requests about the color they want.

Play-dough recipe: Mix two cups of flour, two cups of water and one teaspoon of food coloring in a saucepan. Cook over medium heat, stirring constantly, until dough pulls away from the sides of the pan. Remove the dough from the pan. When it is cool to the touch, knead it for a few minutes. Store in an airtight container.

**Script:** How many of you have played with play-dough before? Great! That's what we are going to do this morning. Did you know that the Bible talks about play-dough? Actually, the prophet Isaiah talks about clay. But clay and play-dough are basically the same thing.

Can you make a shape with your play-dough? Maybe a snake, a heart, or a smooth ball. Show me what you've made. (*Give children a little bit of time to shape the play-dough.*)

I want you to hold your play-dough in the palm of your hand like this. (*Hold the play-dough on your open palm.*) Can your play-dough shape itself into something without your help? Can your play-dough say, "I want to be an airplane" and then magically become an airplane? No way! The play-dough needs someone to shape it. A potter does just that. A potter shapes play-dough. You are the potter for your play-dough. You are in charge of using your hands to shape your play-dough.

Here's what Isaiah said about play-dough in the Bible. Hold your play-dough in the palm of your hand again. Repeat after me:

"I am like this play-dough." (*Give time for the children to repeat what you say.*)

"God is the Potter." (*Children repeat.*)

"God is in charge of me." (*Children repeat.*)

"I am being shaped by God . . . (*Children repeat.*)

"into the person God wants me to be." (*Children repeat.*)

"I cannot shape myself." (*Children repeat.*)

"Only God, my Potter, can shape me." (*Children repeat.*)

Great job! That's exactly what Isaiah said. Every time you play with play-dough, I want you to remember that God is your Potter. He is shaping you into the person he wants you to be. God has wonderful plans for your life.

Let's pray together. Dear God, you are my Potter. I am play-dough in your hands. Shape me into the person you want me to be. I love you! Amen.

**Field Experience:** This children's sermon has the potential to lead to "prop pandemonium"—with play-dough flying and children so distracted it's impossible to get their attention again. Have a good plan in place to deal with discipline issues. If things get out of control, ask the children to put their play-dough between their hands, close their mouths, and put their eyes on you. Wait until everyone is quiet before continuing.

Be sure to have some helpers pick up any dropped play-dough as the children are dismissed. If your church has carpeting, you will find it easier to remove play-dough after it has dried.

**Other Children's Sermon Possibilities:** Hard, dried-out play-dough makes another great prop for a children's sermon. It cannot be shaped into anything. It's useless. When we resist God's commands, when we insist on getting our own way, we become like dried-out play-dough. Incorporate this biblical text from Proverbs 28:14: "Blessed is the man who always fears the LORD, but he who hardens his heart falls into trouble."

**Bible Text:** Joshua 3:1–4:7

**Message:** Remembering God's miracles in the past helps us to trust him in the present.

**Preparation:** You will need a scrapbook, twelve large rocks, and enough small rocks to pass out to the children.

**Script:** I brought a scrapbook with me this morning. (*Hold up the scrapbook and open it for the children to see.*) Inside it there are lots of pictures of my children when they were little. I bet you have a scrapbook of your baby pictures, don't you? From time to time, I like to pull out this scrapbook and flip through the pages because I forget what my children looked like when they were little. This scrapbook helps me to remember all the cute things they did and the fun times we had together as a family.

Many years ago, God wanted his people to remember a special miracle. They did not have scrapbooks or cameras back then. So to help the people remember what happened, God told them to use rocks. (*Hold up a rock.*) That sounds funny to us, doesn't it? Let me explain what I mean.

God was ready to take the people into the Promised Land. But first, there was a river they had to cross: the Jordan River. God told all the people to line up behind the priests who were carrying the ark of the covenant, a special chest containing the Ten Commandments that the priests carried on their shoulders. When the priests got to the river's edge and their toes touched the water, God miraculously stopped the water from flowing. It piled up in a heap, creating a dry path for the people to walk across to the other side of the river. It was amazing!

God wanted the people to remember this miracle. He wanted them to know that he would always take care of them. So God told the leaders of the twelve tribes of Israel to go back to the dry path in the middle of the river and find one rock to bring with them. (*Hold up a rock.*) That's exactly what they did. Each of the twelve leaders picked up one rock from the dry riverbed and carried it to the other side of the Jordan River. The leaders stacked the twelve rocks up in a pile. (*Put the rocks in a pile.*) From that time on, those twelve rocks reminded the people of Israel about God's miracle at the Jordan River. In fact, every time a family traveled by that place, the children would say, "Mom, Dad, why are those rocks stacked up like that?" (*Point to the pile of rocks.*) And the parents would tell their children the story of God's miracle.

I am going to give you a rock today (*hold up a small rock*) to help you remember this story. I want you to put it in your room where you can see it every day. I want you to remember that you can trust God to take care of you today because he has always taken care of his people in the past.

Let's pray together. Dear God, we remember your miracles. We know that you have always taken care of your people. We trust you to take care of us today. We love you, Lord. Amen.

**Field Experience:** Landscape stores are a good place to find rocks of various sizes. You may want to use a wagon to haul the rocks into the sanctuary for the children's sermon. Watch for little fingers as you make your pile of twelve rocks!

**Take-Home Component:** Give parents a handout with instructions for creating a "Spiritual Scrapbook" for their children. This scrapbook could include:

- Pictures of the child at church
- Favorite Bible stories and songs
- Special prayers
- Questions about God
- Pictures of the child celebrating Christmas and Easter
- A record of the child's baptism and first communion.

## The Very Best Book

**Bible Text:** 2 Timothy 3:16–17

**Message:** The Bible is the very best book because it contains God's words for us.

**Preparation:** Gather four or five books that are popular with children of various ages (see script below for suggestions). Put the children's books in a plain box. Put a children's Bible in a fancy box.

**Script:** Some of my favorite things in the whole world are books. Do you like books? Do you like to read books or have books read to you? That's great. There are a lot of good books we can read. I have brought some with me this morning to show you.

(*Pull the first book out of the plain box.*) Do you know the name of this book? It's *Goodnight Moon*. Raise your hand if you have read this book. (*Pull another book out of the box.*)

What's this book? It's *The Very Hungry Caterpillar*. At the end of this book, what does the caterpillar turn into? A beautiful butterfly. (*Continue this process with all the books.*) These are all good books to read. But none of these books is the very best book. There is only one book that is the very best book. (*Open the fancy box and pull out a children's Bible.*) What is this? The Bible. The Bible is the very best book in the whole world because it contains God's words for us. God wanted us to know about the world he created. He wanted us to know how special he made each one of us, how much he loves us, and how he wants us to live. So God gave his words and stories to people, and those people carefully wrote them down to make all the words and stories we have in the Bible today. If you want to know about God, you can read the Bible. If you want to know how to live, you can read the Bible. If you want to know what will happen in the future, you can read the Bible. The Bible is not like these other books because only the Bible tells us God's exact words for us.

Let me ask you a question. Do you have your own Bible at your house? Do you like to read the Bible or have the Bible read to you by your parents? I sure hope so . . . because God wants kids like you to know all about him. If you don't have your own Bible at home, ask your parents to buy one for you. If you do have a Bible of your own, ask your parents to read it with you. Will you do that?

Let's pray together. Thank you, God, for the Bible. It is the very best book in the whole world. Thank you for the stories that teach us about you. We love you, Lord. Amen.

**Field Experience:** You may want to talk to children and parents about the books they like before you pull this children's sermon together. There's nothing worse than thinking something is cool for kids only to find it doesn't match the children's "cool" list. Never assume you know; doing a little research here can go a long way.

**Other Children's Sermon Possibilities:** Use the "surprise bag" technique with Bible stories to keep children's attention and create anticipation as the story moves along. Hide props for the story in a bag, box, or basket and slowly pull them out as the story progresses.

## The Way to Get to Heaven

**Bible Texts:** Romans 3:23; 5:8

**Message:** The way to get to heaven is by believing in Jesus.

**Preparation:** You will need a tall stepladder.

**Script:** Today we're going to talk about how we can get to heaven. When we think about heaven, we think of it as being up in the sky. Using our imaginations, let's pretend that this ladder leads up to heaven. I need a volunteer who is willing to climb this ladder. (*Choose an older volunteer or enlist a responsible child in advance.*)

We may think that we can get to heaven by being good. (*To the child*) Let's imagine some of the good things you might do:

- You obey your parents when they tell you to clean up your room. (*Direct the child to move up one step on the ladder.*)

- You share your new toy with your friend. (*Direct the child to move up one more step on the ladder.*)
- You give the remote control to your sister and let her decide what television show you'll watch. That's really good! (*Direct the child to move up two steps on the ladder.*)

This is really great. All of these good deeds seem to be getting you closer and closer to heaven. The problem is that in addition to doing good things, we *also* do bad things. Romans 3:23 (NLT) says, "For all have sinned; all fall short of God's glorious standard." So let's imagine some of the bad things you might do:

- Maybe you push a friend who cuts in line in front of you. (*Direct the child to come down one step on the ladder.*)
- Maybe you talk back to your parents when they ask you to do something. (*Direct the child to come down one more step on the ladder.*)
- Maybe you tell a little bitty lie. (*Direct the child to come down one more step on the ladder.*)

To try to make up for the bad things you've done, maybe you try even harder to do more and more good things:

- You take out the trash without being asked. (*The child moves up one step.*)
- You are friendly to a new kid at school. (*The child moves up another step.*)
- You put some of your allowance money in the offering plate at church. (*The child moves up another step.*)

But no matter how many good things you do, you also do some bad things. We all do! (*Direct the child to come down a step or two.*)

At this rate, you'll *never* get to heaven. You are stuck—going up and coming down, up and down. God loves us too much to leave us stuck like this. (*Direct the child to come down from the ladder and sit down.*) He wants all of us to get to heaven to live with him forever. So God fixed our problem; he sent Jesus to earth to take the punishment for the bad things we do. This means that when God looks at us, he sees the goodness of Jesus. The Bible says we have been made right in God's sight by the blood of Jesus. This means that the way we get to heaven is by believing in Jesus. He is the only way. But this doesn't mean you should stop doing good things. We follow God's rules every day because we want to show him how much we love him.

Let's thank God for giving us a sure way to get to heaven. Dear God, thank you for sending Jesus to earth so we can get to heaven. We believe in him. We love you, Lord. Amen.

**Field Experience:** When I delivered this children's sermon, the boy who was on the ladder came all the way down, without my prompting, as soon as I started talking about the bad things we do. The congregation laughed. I said something like, "Wow, you must have done some really crazy things!" It was a priceless moment that illustrated the honesty of children. It set the stage to deliver the message of grace and salvation to this young boy and the rest of the congregation. It is important to stay open to these unplanned moments, respond to them, and if possible, incorporate them into the message.

**Other Children's Sermon Possibilities:** Because children are such concrete thinkers, they have a strong sense of fairness and right and wrong. Good people get good things. Bad people get bad things. While holding up the importance of good behavior, we need to shape their thinking to understand the concept of grace: getting something we do not deserve. The story of the thief on the cross is a great one to use for teaching the concept of grace to children.

## Your Secret Weapon

**Bible Texts:** Psalm 50:15; 145:18; 2 Corinthians 12:9–10

**Message:** God strengthens us so we can endure difficult situations.

**Preparation:** You will need a large tug-of-war rope for this children's sermon. Make sure you have enough room to stretch it out completely. You can either stage this children's sermon across the front of your sanctuary or down an aisle. You need to have several adult volunteers ready to help you. These volunteers must be strong enough to pull on the tug-of-war rope and win decisively.

**Script:** (*Stretch out the rope as children are arriving.*) I have a tug-of-war rope with me today. I need one person to stand at this end. (*Choose the smallest child who volunteers.*) I need four or five other kids to stand at the other end. (*Choose the larger children who volunteer to stand on the opposite end of the rope. It should appear obvious that the small child is going to lose the tug-of-war game.*)

Who do you think is going to lose this game of tug-of-war? That's right (*looking at the small child*) . . . it looks like you are outnumbered. It does not look like you stand a chance of winning this game.

(*Look at all the children.*) Have any of you ever been on the losing side of a game? Have you ever felt like nothing is going your way? Have you ever felt worried, or scared, or sad, or depressed? Have you ever had a fight with your best friend? Has your pet ever run away from home? Has someone you love been very sick or even died? Have you ever gotten a bad grade at school? Jesus said that we would have trouble in this life. All of us face difficulty in life.

But there is good news! When we are in trouble, when we feel outnumbered, when it looks as if we're going to be beaten, we have a secret weapon: the Lord and his strength. (*Direct adult volunteers to stand on the "losing side."*) In the Bible God tells us, "Call upon me in the day of trouble; I will deliver you" (Ps. 50:15). The Bible also says, "The LORD is near to all who call on him" (Ps. 145:18). The apostle Paul teaches us that God's power is made perfect in us when we are weak. Paul said, "I delight in weaknesses, in insults, in hardships, in persecutions, in difficulties. For when I am weak, then I am strong" (2 Cor. 12:10).

(*Play tug-of-war. Then put down the rope and have the volunteers sit down.*)

When you face trouble and it looks as if you're outnumbered and defeated, call on the Lord for help. He is your secret weapon in this life. He will come near to you, just like these adults have come near to (*name of child*), and he will strengthen you to get through any difficulty or sadness or fear you may face.

Let's pray together. Dear God, you are my secret weapon. You are my strength. I will call on you when I am afraid or feeling outnumbered. Thank you for coming near to me in times of trouble. Amen.

**Field Experience:** Be sure to prepare your adult volunteers to put their muscle into the tug-of-war game. One time when I led this children's sermon, the adult side almost lost! The kids on the other side were stronger than we expected.

You do not want the tug-of-war outcome to contradict the message you are trying to teach.

**Other Children's Sermon Possibilities:** Tug-of-war is a great metaphor for spiritual warfare. "God/good" is on one side; the "devil/evil" is on the other side. Sometimes it appears that the devil is winning. We see a lot of evil in our world. But we know that the ultimate victory belongs to God. The enemy of our souls will be defeated.

# 8

## Event-Driven Children's Sermons

### Back to School Blessing

**Bible Text:** Matthew 19:14–15

**Message:** Jesus understands what it is like to go to school.

**Preparation:** Before you call the children forward, explain that you need an adult representative to come down with each child. It can be a parent, a grandparent, or an adult friend. Let the adults know that they will be giving a special blessing to the children this morning. Have several adults on hand that morning to bless any child who does not have a parent present.

**Script:** Good morning, everyone! It's that time of year again—back to school. Raise your hand if you have already gone back to school. Wow! That's great. I want to find out what grade all of you are in. If you're in fifth grade, stand up and wave. (*Wait for the fifth graders to stand up.*) Okay, fifth graders, sit down. If you're in fourth grade, stand up and wave . . . (*continue this process all the way down to preschoolers*).

Did you know that Jesus understands what it is like to go to school? When he was a boy, just about your age, he went to school too. Jesus knows what it is like to take a test and have homework. He knows how it feels to have a new teacher and meet new friends. Jesus understands what it is like to be a kid because he was a kid too.

When Jesus became an adult, he did something very special to show children that he cared about them. Jesus blessed them. Jesus put his hands on children like this (*put your hand on a child's head*) and spoke loving words to them. That's called a blessing.

Since you are at the start of a new school year, we want to bless each of you just as Jesus blessed the children. So I'm going to ask all of you to stand up and spread out a little bit. (*Allow time for the children to do this.*) Now I need your parents or grandparents or aunts or uncles or friends or whoever brought you to church today to stand by you and lay their hands on you. (*Allow time for the parents to gather around their children. If some parents did not come forward with their children, give time for them to come forward now. Make sure each child has an adult before you proceed!*)

Parents and friends, I want you to whisper a special blessing to your child. I want you to bless him or her by saying three things:

1. I love you.
2. God loves you.
3. God has special plans for your year at school.

Now I want all the children to get on their knees. Parents and friends, put your hands on them one more time and I will pray. Father God, you love these children. They belong to you. We lift them up to you as they begin a new year of school. Help them to learn about the world you have made. Give them wisdom to make good decisions. Show them how to love the other children in their class and to honor their teachers. Protect them, Lord. In Jesus's name we pray, amen.

**Field Experience:** Since parents are very important in this children's sermon, I would publicize to families what you are planning to do several weeks in advance. You may even provide parents with a brief description of what will happen.

**Other Children's Sermon Possibilities:** Going back to school is a big deal in the lives of families. You can also talk about how to handle first-day jitters, homework, getting along with friends and teachers.

## Going to the Doctor

**Bible Text:** Hebrews 12:11

**Message:** Discipline is painful at first, but it will make our lives better as we grow up.

**Preparation:** You will need a child-size doctor's kit with equipment inside.

**Script:** All of us have to go to the doctor sometimes. Often we get sick and we visit the doctor so that he or she can help us get better. Other times, we may go to the doctor for a checkup. We're not sick; we're just getting our bodies checked to make sure everything is working the right way.

I have some equipment a doctor might use at a checkup. (*Pull the items out of the kit as you go.*) This is a stethoscope. What does the doctor do with this? The doctor listens to your heartbeat. This is a blood pressure cuff. The doctor puts this on your arm to check how your blood is flowing. This is an otoscope. The doctor uses this to look deep inside your ear to make sure there are no kitty cats in there . . . or infections either.

Now none of this stuff (*hold up the equipment*) hurts, does it? But there is one thing that sometimes happens at the doctor's office that does hurt. What is that? (*Listen to responses.*) Getting a shot! Oweee! Whether you get a shot in your arm or in your backside—it hurts. Shots are not fun, but they are important. Shots put medicine into our bodies to protect us from really bad diseases. Shots hurt at first, but they help us to stay healthy later in life.

The Bible says there is something else that hurts at first and then makes us better. Listen carefully to this Bible verse: "No discipline is enjoyable while it is happening—it is painful!" (Heb. 12:11 NLT). (*Be sure to emphasize the word* discipline *as you read this verse.*) What is painful? Discipline is painful at the time it is happening. When we disobey our parents, they have to discipline us. It is not fun. It's painful to go to time-out or have a privilege taken away or maybe even get a spanking. But being disciplined, even though it is hard at first, helps us have a better life in the future. It's just like getting shots: They're painful, but then we are better for the rest of our lives. The Bible says, "Afterward there will be a quiet harvest of right living for those who are trained in this way" (Heb. 12:11 NLT).

When our parents discipline us, they are teaching us the right way to live so when we get older we will make wise choices on our own. Our parents discipline us because they love us. It may seem painful to us at first, but our parents' discipline will help us live wisely later in life.

Let's put our hands together and close our eyes to pray. Dear God, I do not like to be disciplined. It makes me sad at the time it is happening. But I thank you that my parents love me enough to discipline me. Help me to learn the lessons they are trying to teach me. In Jesus's name, amen.

**Field Experience:** If you have a pediatrician in your congregation, ask the person to come in a lab coat and bring some of the instruments that he or she uses to examine children. Be sure to have a microphone so the doctor can be heard.

**Other Children's Sermon Possibilities:** Sin is like a germ that infects us and makes us "sick." Talk about confession and repentance as medicine for dealing with our sin sickness.

## I-want-itis

**Bible Text**: Luke 12:13–21

**Message:** Jesus teaches us to be on guard against greed.

**Preparation:** None

**Script:** Do children ever get sick? You bet! What are some of the sicknesses that you have gotten? (*Listen to the children's responses. Add some of your own if necessary: ear infections, colds, stomachaches, sore throats, laryngitis, tonsillitis, bronchitis.*) When you get any of these sicknesses, you should stay home from school, go to the doctor, and take medicine. Being sick is not fun.

I have noticed that a lot of kids get another sickness called "I-want-itis." Say that with me . . . "I-want-itis." This disease affects many, many children. In fact, you might have it and not even know it. Let me describe it to you:

- When you go to the grocery store, the toy store, or even the drugstore, do you see a lot of things that you want to buy? Do you constantly say to your mom, "Ooh, I want that. I want this. Please, I really want it"?

- When you watch commercials on television, do they make you say over and over again, "I want that"?

- When you go to a friend's birthday party and your friend opens the presents, do you say to yourself, "I want that too"?

- Do you have a long, long list of all the things you want for Christmas?

- Do you behave like a crazy person when you do not get the things you want? Do you whine, cry, throw yourself onto the ground, pout, plead, and beg?

Oh dear, this is terrible. I think all of you may have a case of "I-want-itis." The bad news is that your doctor cannot help you with this disease. The good news is that the Bible has the cure we need.

Jesus said in Luke 12:15, "Be on your guard against all kinds of greed." That's what "I-want-itis" is: greed. Greed is the constant feeling of wanting things. Jesus tells us that we have to be on guard, to watch out, when greediness starts creeping into our lives. Jesus also said that life is not about having a lot of things. Toys are fun to play with, but they are not the most important thing in life. God is the most important thing in life.

This means that when your I-want-itis flares up, you may need to turn off the television or stop hanging out at the mall. You may need to run around outside or pull out the toys you *do* have and play with them. You could even pray and ask God to help you feel content with what you have instead of wanting more and more things. I-want-itis can be a serious problem for children, and adults too, but God can make us better.

Let's pray together. Dear God, there are so many things we want. Sometimes our greedy feelings get overwhelming. Help us to be happy with what we have. Teach us to want more and more of you. We love you, Lord. Amen.

**Field Experience:** Children sometimes have a tendency to deny that they do anything wrong. If you ask children if they have "I-want-itis" and they say "Not me," have a little fun by turning to the congregation and asking, "Parents, do you think your children may get a mild case of 'I-want-itis' from time to time?" They will certainly respond, "Yes!"

**Other Children's Sermon Possibilities:** The "Parable of the Rich Fool" is another great story to tell to children about the pitfalls of greedy living. Consider scheduling a used toy drive to give children a tangible way to give their toys to deserving children.

**Bible Text:** Romans 6:23

**Message:** God's gift of eternal life through Jesus lasts forever.

**Preparation:** You will need a large whiteboard, a dry-erase marker, an eraser, and a permanent marker. Cover the whiteboard in removable clear vinyl. This will protect the whiteboard from the permanent marker.

**Script:** Christmastime is almost here. I bet a lot of you are thinking about your Christmas presents. Today I want us to talk about who gives the very best Christmas presents.

*(Write "Parents" at the top of one side of the whiteboard with a dry-erase marker.)* Our parents give us Christmas presents, don't they? What are some presents your parents might get you for Christmas this year? *(Write down five or six of the children's responses under "Parents.")*

*(Write "Santa Claus" at the top of the other side of the whiteboard with a dry-erase marker.)* You may have also heard about Santa Claus, who brings presents to good boys and girls. What are some of the presents Santa Claus might bring you this year? *(Write down five or six of the children's responses under "Santa Claus.")*

*(Write "God" at the top of the whiteboard in between "Parents" and "Santa Claus." Use permanent marker.)* We all know that Christmas is about a special present that God has given to us. The Bible says: "The free gift of God is eternal life through Christ Jesus our Lord" (Rom. 6:23 NLT). *(Write "Eternal Life through Jesus" in permanent marker under "God.")* This means if we believe in Jesus, we will go

to heaven to live with God when our life on earth is over. We will live with him forever and ever.

Now, our parents and Santa Claus can give us some pretty good presents, but those presents are not the best. They will eventually wear out (*slowly start erasing the presents listed under "Parents" and "Santa Claus"*) or we'll get tired of playing with them. Those presents will not make us happy forever. They just will not last. But God's present of eternal life through Jesus lasts forever. (*Attempt to erase "Eternal Life through Jesus."*) It cannot be broken or taken away from us. This means that Jesus is the best Christmas present we could ever receive.

Let's thank God for Jesus. Dear God, thank you for giving us Jesus that very first Christmas. Your present of eternal life is the best. We love you, Lord. Amen.

**Field Experience:** What if a child calls out "My mom said there is no such thing as Santa Claus"? How will you handle this situation in front of the other children? I would probably say something like, "That is something you need to talk to your mom and dad about when you get home."

**Other Children's Sermon Possibilities:** Use the whiteboard and markers to teach a lesson about how God forgives our sin and remembers it no more (see Jer. 31:34). Write various sins on the board. Tell children that Jesus is like an eraser. Jesus takes away our sins so that God does not remember them anymore.

# Losing Your Teeth

**Bible Text:** Matthew 10:39

**Message:** Jesus wants us to focus on him instead of ourselves.

**Preparation:** None

**Script:** This morning I need to see your teeth. Will you show them to me? Wow, your teeth look pretty good. Do any of you have a tooth that is loose? Can you wiggle it for me? How many of you have lost a tooth? Losing teeth is something that will happen to all of you. As you grow, you will outgrow your baby teeth and they will fall out and be replaced by new, big teeth that you will have for the rest of your life—hopefully!

When you lose a tooth, is it really sad? Do you cry about it and get upset? Do you hang on to that tooth and try to stick it back into your mouth? Not usually. How do you feel when you lose a tooth? Happy! Why do you feel happy? Maybe because the tooth fairy comes. And why does it make you happy that the tooth fairy comes? Because she leaves you money! Now that is something to be happy about . . . you lose a tooth but you get something in return—money!

Jesus talks about something else that we need to lose. He said, "Whoever loses his life for my sake will find it" (Matt. 10:39). Jesus said we need to lose our lives. That means you need to stop worrying about yourself and focus on Jesus. It means not worrying about how many toys you have or want but focusing instead on Jesus. It means not pushing your way to the front of the line or always insisting that you go first but focusing instead on Jesus. We lose our lives when we say to Jesus, "Jesus, you are in charge of me today. I will do what you want me to do, when you want me to do it."

When we lose a tooth, we receive something from the tooth fairy. When we lose our lives for Jesus, we get something in return—a better life than we could ever imagine. You see, Jesus is in charge of life on this earth. And when we live his way, we receive a full and wonderful life. Jesus is also in charge of life in heaven. When we lose our lives and focus on him, he promises us that we will receive rewards in heaven.

If you want to lose your life and live instead for Jesus, repeat this prayer: Dear Jesus, you are in charge of me today and every day. I will do what you want me to do, when you want me to do it. I love you. Amen.

**Field Experience:** This children's sermon is a little dangerous because it can encourage a lot of talking on the part of the children. They may all want to tell you how many teeth they have lost and exactly how much money the tooth fairy has left them . . . or that they haven't lost any teeth at all . . . or that their teeth got knocked out on the playground. Let them verbalize in ways that are appropriate, then "nip it" if things get too chatty. I get chatter under control by saying things like, "Can you tell me more about that when I've finished talking?" or "That's great; now it's my turn to talk and your turn to listen."

**Other Children's Sermon Possibilities:** Giving up ourselves is a tough concept to explain to children but one that we must not shy away from. Concepts such as putting others first (Mark 9:35) and giving instead of receiving (Acts 20:35) are critical building blocks in the life of discipleship. During the formative years of childhood, we must teach these principles, even though they collide with what seems fair in the minds of children.

**Bible Text:** Psalm 139:7–10

**Message:** God is with you wherever you go.

**Preparation:** None

**Script:** School is out for the summer. How do you feel about that? I bet you are feelin' great. Raise your hand if you are doing something special or going on a trip this summer. Where are you going? (*Accept responses from several children.*)

I have great news for all of you who are traveling this summer. God will be with you wherever you go. That's what the Bible says in Psalm 139:7–10. Stand up with me, and let's learn these Bible verses together. I want you to do whatever I do.

The psalmist says:

"Where can I go from [you, God]? Where can I flee from your presence?"

(*Raise your hands and shrug your shoulders as if asking a question.*)

"If I go up to the heavens (*stretch up as tall as you can*), [God,] you are there."

"If I make my bed in the depths (*lie down flat on the ground*), [God,] you are there."

"If I rise on the wings of the dawn (*stand up and face east*), [God, you are there]."

"If I settle on the far side of the sea (*turn and face west*), [God, you are there]."

"Even there your hand will guide me (*hold up your hands, cupped together*); [God, you hold me in your hands]."

Let's sit down. You did a great job. Wherever you go this summer—up, down, east, west, to the beach, to the mountains, to a theme park, or to the tent pitched in your own backyard—God will be with you. God never takes a vacation from you!

Repeat this prayer after me. Dear God, I praise you. You are with me wherever I go. Thank you for never leaving me. Amen.

**Field Experience:** When I delivered this children's sermon, one child told me she was going to the south of France for a month for her summer vacation. We all oohed and aahed. At the same time, it's important to be sensitive to children who may not have such elaborate plans for the summer. Taking a trip to a theme park or lake, visiting Grandma's house, going to the movie theater, or spending the night with friends—all of these count as "vacation."

In addition, this children's sermon requires a lot of movement. Be sure you are dressed appropriately for stretching up tall, lying on the ground, and gracefully getting back to your feet again.

**Other Children's Sermon Possibilities:** Create a summer series called "Hot Bible Stories." Stories should all include some heat: "Moses and the Burning Bush"; "Elijah and the Prophets of Baal"; "Shadrach, Meshach, and Abednego"; and "Pentecost."

**Bible Text:** John 3:16

**Message:** There are lots of opposites in the Easter story.

**Preparation:** Make four booklets of opposite words as outlined below—one word per page. I recommend having the booklets spiral bound to make it easy for volunteers to flip through the pages.

> Booklet #1: Hot, Cold, Hosanna, Crucify
> Booklet #2: Day, Night, Perfect, Punished
> Booklet #3: Yes, No, Dead, Alive
> Booklet #4: Rich, Poor, The End, The Beginning

**Script:** Do you know what opposites are? Opposites are things that are different from each other in every way. Today we are going to play a game of opposites. I need four volunteers to hold these signs. (*Select four children to hold the flip books.*) We will look at a word, and you can tell me its opposite. Let's get started.

(*Have the first child turn over the first page of his or her book.*) This word is *hot*. What is the opposite of hot? Cold. (*Have the first child turn over the second page of his or her book to reveal the word* cold. *Use the same process with the other three volunteers and their opposite words, revealing only the first set of opposites in each book.*)

Did you know that the story of Easter found in the Bible has a lot of opposites in it? Let me tell you what I mean. On Palm Sunday, Jesus rode into the city of Jerusalem on a donkey. People lined the streets to see him pass by. They put their coats on the ground to make a carpet for the donkey to walk on. They waved palm branches in the air.

They shouted, "Hosanna!" to Jesus (*flip to page 3 of book #1*). The people were so happy to see him.

But just a few days later, when Jesus was arrested, a ruler in Jerusalem asked the crowd of people what they wanted him to do to Jesus. This crowd, which was so excited to see Jesus a few days before, was now completely different. This time, the people shouted, "Crucify!" (*flip to page 4 of book #1*). They wanted Jesus to die.

This is really unbelievable, because Jesus was the only perfect person who ever lived on earth (*flip to page 3 of book #2*). Jesus was like a regular person in every way except that he never did anything wrong. And yet Jesus was punished for the things that other people, including you and me, do wrong. He was perfect, but he was punished (*flip to page 4 of book #2*).

And so Jesus was crucified. His body was nailed to a cross, and he died. His friends took his body down from the cross and placed it in a tomb. Jesus was dead (*flip to page 3 of book #3*). But just a few days later, Jesus was alive again (*flip to page 4 of book #3*). You see, Jesus had God's power in him. God's power is more powerful than anything, including death. So Jesus came back to life to show God's power.

That's not all. There is one more important opposite of the Easter story that you need to know. The Bible tells us that one day our lives on earth will come to an end (*flip to page 3 of book #4*). We will die. But if we believe in Jesus, by God's power, we will come alive again in heaven, where we will live forever. Death is not the end of our lives. Just the opposite is true. Death is the beginning of our life in heaven (*flip to page 4 of book #4*).

Let's pray together. Dear God, it is amazing how you work in the opposites of life. Thank you for the story of Easter. Thank you for sending Jesus to earth. You are awesome, God. Amen.

**Field Experience:** I think some of the hardest sermons to create are those on the topics of Christmas and Easter. These events are so theologically significant that we can be tempted to say too much at one time. I think the best tactic is to isolate a fresh way to tell the Easter or Christmas story that answers the question: "Why is this celebration so important to us?"

**Other Children's Sermon Possibilities:** The New Testament story of Lazarus is another account that seems to have a bad ending until Jesus shows up and raises him from the dead. The Old Testament story of Joseph follows a similar structure. For these stories, you could make cue cards that say "That was good" and "That was bad." Hold up the cue card throughout the story, asking the children to say what is written on the card. The message: God can make good things come out of bad situations.

## Valentine's Day Cards

**Bible Text:** Matthew 5:44–48

**Message:** Jesus commands us to love people who are difficult to love.

**Preparation:** Purchase several valentines based on the script below. If you find other interesting cards, substitute your own choices. Pick cards that have a brief, child-friendly text. Create three cards for the people who are hard to love. Use construction paper and decorate them. Put the title on the outside of the card. Handwrite or type the text inside each card.

**Script:** Valentine's Day is just around the corner. One way we celebrate Valentine's Day is by giving cards to the people we love. I went to the card store the other day to shop for cards. I was amazed at all the different kinds of cards you can buy. There are cards for your parents. (*Hold up one and read the message.*) There are cards for teachers. (*Hold it up and read it.*) You can even get a card for your pet. (*Hold it up and read it.*)

But there were some cards I just couldn't find. I couldn't find any cards for people who are hard for me to love. Jesus said we are to love people even when they are not loving or nice to us. So I made some cards for people who are hard to love.

Here's one for "My Annoying Brother." Do any of you have a brother or sister who gets on your nerves? Listen to what this card says:

> You take my toys
> And make lots of noise.
> Sometimes your socks smell bad.
> When mom turns her back,
> You give me a smack.
> When I get in trouble, you're glad.
> But somewhere down deep
> You're a brother to keep.
> A friend you'll always be.
> So even though
> You annoy me so,
> I love you, can't you see?

Or how about someone who makes fun of you or picks on you? This card is for "The Bully at My School."

155

You point your finger and call me names,
You never pick me for playground games.
If I trip or stumble, you laugh out loud,
You seem to be in the popular crowd.
But I am guessing that you hurt too
And that you don't like people laughing at you.
Because I love Jesus, I can be your friend.
Maybe together, we both can win.

And finally, do you have an ex–best friend? Is there someone who used to be your best friend, but now you don't get along? Here's the perfect card for "My Ex–Best Friend."

The best of friends we used to be,
Always together, you and me.
But then we argued and were very rude,
Our friendship seemed to come unglued.
I am missing you on Valentine's Day.
I know that Jesus wants me to say,
"Can we forgive each other and start again?
I'd like you back as my best friend."

There are some people who are hard for us to love. We need to ask God to help us. Let's do that right now. Dear God, it is hard for us to love people who have hurt our feelings. Sometimes it is hard for us to love the people in our own family. Help us, Lord. Fill us up with your love so we have plenty to give to other people. Amen.

**Field Experience:** This children's sermon requires the children to do a lot of listening. My experience is that they pay close attention to this topic because it hits so close to reality for many of them. Be animated when you are reading the cards and keep the pace moving.

**Other Children's Sermon Possibilities:** Children often latch on to the concept of fairness in dealing with people and life situations. The old "she hit me first" excuse for misbehavior is a case in point. We can help children to mature in discipleship by giving them the freedom to feel the emotions of life's unfairness while at the same time holding up the standard Jesus sets for our behavior. When children are feeling angry or hurt or frustrated, teach them to use prayer as a strategy for dealing with their emotions. The "Parable of the Prodigal Son" (focused on the older son) is another great story to illustrate how mercy is more important in God's kingdom than fairness.

## What Freedom Means

**Bible Text:** John 8:31–34

**Message:** Jesus sets us free from sin.

**Preparation:** You will need strips of cloth.

**Script:** Today is the Fourth of July (or, this week we'll be celebrating the Fourth of July). It's a day when we celebrate freedom. I want to teach you what we, as followers of Jesus Christ, believe freedom means.

There are some kids who think that freedom means getting to do whatever they feel like doing whenever they feel like doing it. There are some kids who think that freedom means having no rules to follow—no rules from parents, no rules at school, no rules from God.

But that is not the life of freedom; that is the life of sin. When we do whatever we want to do without consideration for our parents' rules or our school rules or God's rules—that is sin. Sin traps us. Jesus said it this way in John 8:34: "Everyone who sins is a slave to sin." I need a brave volunteer to help me show you exactly what Jesus means. (*Choose a volunteer to stand up with you in front of the other children.*)

If we use our eyes to watch ungodly television shows or movies or play violent video games, we are not free. (*Tie a strip of cloth securely around the child's eyes.*) Our eyes are tied up with sin. If we use our mouths to say whatever words we feel like saying—bad words, unkind words, or gossip about another person—we are not free. (*Tie a strip of cloth carefully around the child's mouth. Be sure he or she can still breathe!*) Our mouths are tied up in sin. When we hit, push, or take what doesn't belong to us, we are not free. (*Tie a strip of cloth around the child's hands.*) Our hands are tied up in sin. If we use our feet to walk into tempting situations or to walk away from someone who needs help because we don't feel like helping, we are not free. (*Make sure the child maintains balance while you tie a strip of cloth around his or her feet.*) Our feet are tied up in sin. This is what Jesus meant when he said, "Everyone who sins is a slave to sin."

Here's the real problem with sin. Can you get yourself free? (*Ask the volunteer. Let him or her attempt to get untied.*) No way! You cannot set yourself free from sin. Only Jesus can do that. Jesus died on the cross to free us from our sins. Jesus sets us free to use our eyes to see and enjoy the wonderful things he has made in the world. (*Untie the cloth around the child's eyes.*) Jesus sets us free to use our mouths to praise his name and to encourage other people. (*Untie the cloth around the child's mouth.*) Jesus sets us free to use our hands to hug, to help, and to serve other people. (*Untie the cloth around the child's hands.*) Jesus sets us free to use our feet to follow his plans for our lives. (*Untie the cloth around the child's feet.*)

In 2 Corinthians 3:17 the Bible says, "Where the Spirit of the Lord is, there is freedom." This Fourth of July, as we celebrate freedom, I want you to remember that true freedom comes from Jesus and following his commands for our life.

Let's pray together. Dear God, following you is the way to freedom. Help us to understand and believe this. Help us to obey you. In Jesus's name, amen.

**Field Experience:** The first time I did this children's sermon, the boy I tied up started to wiggle loose on his own. I had to ask him to stay still and cooperate with me! The second time I did this children's sermon, I prepped my volunteer in advance so he would not try to wiggle loose just to get a laugh from the congregation. It worked much better! Also, take care not to tie the knots so tightly that untying them is difficult.

**Take-Home Component:** I put together a "Christian Flag-Making Kit" to pass out to each child at the end of the children's sermon. It included the supplies and directions to put together a flag that reminded them of the freedom they have in Christ.

## Who Has a Birthday?

**Bible Texts:** Genesis 1:1; Revelation 22:13

**Message:** God is eternal.

159

**Preparation:** You need to wear a birthday hat and carry in some helium balloons. You can have hats to pass out to the kids to wear during the children's sermon.

**Script:** Today we are celebrating birthdays. (*Pass out the party hats.*) Your birthday is the day you were born. It is the day your life on earth began. If you were born in the month of January, please stand up. Happy Birthday! If your birthday is in February, stand up. Happy Birthday! (*Continue calling out all the months.*) I hope everyone here has a happy birthday.

Did you know that God does not have a birthday? The Bible tells us that God has always been here. God does not have a beginning. I know it is hard for us to understand, but God was never born. He has always existed. And furthermore, God will always exist. God does not have an end.

You and I have a day when we were born and we will have a day when we will die. That is not true of God. God has always been and will always be. God is eternal. Say that word with me: "Eternal." Eternal means lasting forever. This is one of the many reasons we worship God. God is bigger and better than we are. He has no beginning and no end.

Let's get on our knees and worship him together. Dear God, we worship you because you are eternal. You have always been. You will always be. We love you, God. Amen.

**Field Experience:** Invite the whole congregation to participate in this children's sermon. To add a twist, have everyone stand up, turn around, and sit down on their birthday month. This really gets the blood pumping and helps the children sit still for the rest of the children's sermon.

**Other Children's Sermon Possibilities:** Focus on the birthday of the church by telling children the story of Pentecost, singing "Happy Birthday" to the church, and eating birthday cake after the service.

# 9

# Series-Driven Children's Sermons

## Christmas Night Live

### *Introduction*

For this series of children's sermons, you will be creating a simple live nativity using the children who come forward for the message each week. You will also need a simple stable set—two cardboard or lightweight wood cutouts that can be held by helpers to form the stable—a manger, a stool, a baby doll, a star, a step stool, a cross, a heart cutout, and costumes. Costumes should be easy to put on over the children's clothes. Characters needing costumes include:

- Mary and Joseph
- Angel (one child)
- Shepherds (two children)
- Wise men (three children)

If you want to make it possible for more children to participate, add more angels and shepherds. You will also need some youth or adult helpers to get the children in and out of their costumes quickly.

For added effect, you can make a sign that lights up and reads "LIVE." A talented member of our children's ministry staff created a sign by drilling holes in pieces of wood to form the word *live*. She pulled Christmas lights through the holes. She ran an extension cord to the nearest electrical outlet and plugged in the sign as we got started. An adult will need to hold the sign because the lights can generate heat.

## Christmas Night Live—Mary and Joseph

**Bible Texts:** Luke 1:26–38; Matthew 1:18–25

**Message:** Mary and Joseph said yes to God.

**Preparation:** You will need the "LIVE" sign, the stable cutouts, costumes for Mary and Joseph, a stool for Mary to sit on, and the manger.

**Script:** (*Have your volunteers stand in place with the stable cutouts.*) Hello, everyone! Christmas is coming. For the next five weeks, we are going to be re-creating the story of the first Christmas piece by piece. We're calling it "Christmas Night Live!" (*Turn on the sign.*) Today we are learning about Mary and Joseph. Is there anyone here who will be Mary and Joseph? You just need to wear a costume and say one word out loud. (*Select a male and female volunteer and have them stand in front with you.*)

The Bible doesn't tell us a lot about Mary and Joseph. We can assume that they were just ordinary people like you and me. They were not rich. They were not famous. They were not supersmart. They did not have any spectacular talents or abilities. Mary and Joseph were very ordinary. But God chose them to do something very extraordinary. God asked Mary and Joseph to be Jesus's parents while he lived on earth.

God sent an angel to talk to Mary first. (*Begin to dress Mary.*) The angel told her, "Mary, God has chosen you to be the mother of a very special baby. The baby will be God's Son. He will be great. He will save the world. It's a big job to be his mother. Will you do it?" And Mary said . . . (*look at the volunteer and wait for the volunteer to respond: "Yes!"*). Great! That's exactly what Mary said. She said yes to what God asked her to do. She was an ordinary girl asked to do something extraordinary by God, and she said "Yes!" (*Place Mary in the stable sitting on the stool.*)

Then God sent an angel to talk to Joseph in a dream. (*Begin to dress Joseph.*) The angel told him, "Joseph, God has chosen you to do something very important. Mary, the girl you are going to marry, is pregnant with a special baby. The baby will be God's Son. He will be great. He will save the world. It is a big job to be his father. Will you do it?" And Joseph said . . . (*look at the volunteer and wait for the volunteer to respond: "Yes!"*). Great! The Bible says that when Joseph woke up he did what the angel commanded. He brought Mary home to be his wife. Joseph was an ordinary man asked to do something extraordinary by God, and he said "Yes!" (*Place Joseph in the stable next to Mary.*)

When I think of Mary and Joseph that first Christmas, I think about kids like you. You look like a bunch of ordinary kids to me (*looking at the children*). But I would be willing to bet that God has something special, maybe even something extraordinary, that he wants you to do in your life. Let me ask you a question. When God asks you to do something extraordinary, what are you going to say? (*Children respond: "Yes."*)

Let's pray together. Dear God, like Mary and Joseph, we are ordinary people. And like Mary and Joseph, we are ready to say yes to whatever you ask us to do. We love you, Lord. Amen.

**Field Experience:** What I love about this series is that it involves an ever-increasing number of children every week in a live nativity that requires no rehearsals! The biggest logistical hurdle you will face is getting children into costumes quickly. The more characters you add, the more helpers you'll need. We also prep our music team to play a little "dressing music" if we're struggling to get everyone ready in time.

**Other Children's Sermon Possibilities:** Children learn to say no to their parents at a young age. What happens if they say no to God? The stories of Jonah and the rich young ruler are good examples of people who refused to obey God.

## Christmas Night Live—The Angels

**Bible Text:** Luke 2:8–14

**Message:** The angels praised God.

**Preparation:** You will need the sign, the stable cutouts, costumes for Mary and Joseph, a stool for Mary to sit on, the manger, the step stool, and the angel costume.

**Script:** (*Select child volunteers to come forward to be Mary and Joseph. Get them in costume and put them in their places in the stable.*) Good morning, everyone! We are in the process of re-creating the very first Christmas, piece by piece. We're calling it "Christmas Night Live!" (*Plug in the sign.*) Last week we talked about Mary and Joseph. What did Mary and Joseph say when God asked them to be Jesus's parents on earth? They said "Yes!" Mary and Joseph were ordinary people doing something extraordinary for God.

Today we are talking about the angels. I need one volunteer to be an angel. (*Choose a child and start dressing him or her. Place the angel in the stable on the step stool, behind Mary and Joseph.*) Angels are in a special category in God's creation. They are not exactly like God, but they are not exactly like people either. Angels are somewhere in between. Angels are very important in the Christmas story. We learned last week that angels appeared to both Mary and Joseph to tell them what God had planned. Today we are learning about when the angels appeared to the shepherds on that very first Christmas. The Bible tells us exactly what happened:

"That night some shepherds were in the fields outside the village, guarding their flocks of sheep. Suddenly, an angel of the Lord appeared among them, and the radiance of the Lord's glory surrounded them. [The shepherds] were terribly frightened, but the angel reassured them. 'Don't be afraid!' he said. 'I bring you good news of great joy for everyone! The Savior—yes, the Messiah, the Lord—has been born tonight in Bethlehem, the city of David! And this is how you will recognize him: You will find a baby lying in a manger, wrapped snugly in strips of cloth!' Suddenly, the angel was joined by a vast host of others—the armies of heaven—praising God: 'Glory to God in the highest heaven, and peace on earth to all whom God favors'" (Luke 2:8–14 NLT).

In this part of the Christmas story, angels did two important things. First, the angels delivered a message from God to the shepherds. The message was: "Tonight, the Savior of the world has been born in Bethlehem." The second thing the angels did was to praise God. They told the shepherds, "God is great!" That's what it means to praise God—to give God credit for great things that happen.

Now listen closely . . . we are like angels in one important way. Just like the angels, we can praise God too. In fact, that's one of the reasons God made us—so that we would give him praise. When something great happens in your life, give God the credit. When you get a good grade on a test, say "Praise God." When you are sick and then you get well, say "Praise God." When you have a fun day playing with your friends, say "Praise God." When you're outside and you see something wonderful that God made, say "Praise God." When you snuggle into your bed at night, with food in your tummy and a roof over your head, say "Praise God." Like the angels, you were made to say "Praise God."

Let's pray. Dear God, we praise you! You do great things for us! You sent Jesus to earth to be the Savior of the whole world. We will praise you every day of our lives! Amen.

**Field Experience:** As children become familiar with these children's sermons from week to week, they can fill in the blanks for you. You might say, "Let's review":

Mary and Joseph said _____ ("Yes") to God.
The angels _____ (praised) God.

**Other Children's Sermon Possibilities:** Identify Bible stories that include angels. Pick three to link together in one children's sermon. Pass out halos for the children to wear and ask them to stand up and flap their arms every time they hear the word *angel*.

## Christmas Night Live—The Shepherds

**Bible Text:** Luke 2:15–16

**Message:** The shepherds hurried to find the baby Jesus.

**Preparation:** You will need the sign, the stable cutouts, a stool for Mary to sit on, the manger, the baby doll, the step stool, and costumes for Mary, Joseph, the angel, and the shepherds.

**Script:** (*Select volunteers to be Mary, Joseph, and the angel. Give Mary the baby doll to put in the manger. Get these characters in their places in the stable.*)

Good morning, everyone! We are in the process of re-creating the very first Christmas, piece by piece. We're calling it "Christmas Night Live!" (*Turn on the sign.*) We have talked about Mary and Joseph. What did Mary and Joseph say when God asked them to be Jesus's parents on earth? They said "Yes!" Then we learned about the angels. The angels were very important in the Christmas story. They praised God, which means they gave God credit for doing great things on earth.

Today we are going to learn about the shepherds. I need two people to volunteer to be our shepherds. (*Choose two volunteers and start getting them into their costumes. Then place the shepherds in the stable scene.*) Can anyone tell me what a shepherd's job involves? (*Listen to responses.*) That's right, shepherds take care of sheep. Shepherds take their flocks of sheep from place to place, from field to field in search of grass to eat. At night, they camp out in the fields with the sheep. The shepherds were out in the fields keeping watch over their sheep when the angels appeared to them that very first Christmas. The angels said, "Great news! A Savior for the whole world has been born tonight. You can find the Savior in the town of Bethlehem. You will know that you are at the right place when you find a baby lying in a manger, wrapped snugly in strips of cloth!"

The Bible tells us exactly what the shepherds did after they heard the message from the angels: "[The shepherds] hurried off and found Mary and Joseph, and the baby" (Luke 2:16). Did you hear that? Another Bible version says, "They ran to the village and found Mary and Joseph. And there was the baby" (Luke 2:16 NLT). Shepherds (*to the volunteers*), show me how fast you can run in place. That's fast! The shepherds did not delay to go find the baby Jesus. They did not make excuses or say things like "Let's get a good night's sleep, and in the morning we'll head into town." Instead, they jumped up and ran to find Jesus.

Now I want the rest of you to stand up. Everyone, show me how fast you can run in place. You sure look like fast runners. Sit down, everyone. Just like the shepherds, there is something the Bible tells us we should be in a hurry to do. We should be in a hurry to obey God. Sometimes we like to make excuses instead of obeying. Sometimes we think: *I'll do what God wants me to do later. I don't really feel like doing the right thing right now.* Sometimes we dilly-dally. The Bible teaches us that when we know the right thing to do, we should do it right away. That's what we can learn from the shepherds.

168

Let's pray together. Dear God, sometimes we are slow to obey you. Sometimes we make excuses. Sometimes we don't feel like doing the right thing. Help us to obey right away just like the shepherds. In Jesus's name, amen.

**Field Experience:** You can enhance your shepherd costumes by adding staffs and stuffed animals. You might even pass out candy canes (they look like shepherd staffs) to all the children after the closing prayer.

**Other Children's Sermon Possibilities:** Psalm 23 centers around the metaphor of sheep and shepherds. Have a local shepherd bring a few sheep to church to teach the children what shepherds do. You can bring a sheep into your sanctuary (if you are brave!) or you can set up a petting area somewhere outside. Children will love this hands-on learning experience.

## Christmas Night Live—The Wise Men

**Bible Text:** Matthew 2:9–11

**Message:** The wise men followed the star.

**Preparation:** You will need the sign, the star, the stable cutouts, a stool for Mary to sit on, the manger, the baby doll, the step stool, and costumes for Mary, Joseph, the angel, the shepherds, and the wise men. Hang the star on the stable cutout.

**Script:** (*Select volunteers to be Mary, Joseph, the angel, and the shepherds. Give Mary the baby doll to put in the manger. Get these characters in their places in the stable.*)

Good morning, everyone! We are in the process of re-creating the very first Christmas, piece by piece. We're calling it "Christmas Night Live!" (*Turn on the sign.*) We have talked about Mary and Joseph. What did Mary and Joseph say when God asked them to be Jesus's parents on earth? They said "Yes!" Then we learned about the angels. They praised God, which means they gave God credit for doing great things on earth. Finally, we talked about the shepherds. They hurried; they ran to find the baby Jesus.

Today we are going to learn about the wise men. I need three people to volunteer to be our wise men. (*Choose three volunteers and start getting them into their costumes. Then place them in the stable scene.*) The wise men studied the stars and the planets. They also must have studied the Old Testament, because the Old Testament talks about a new king who would rule the whole earth. The wise men believed that a special star would appear in the sky as a sign that this new king was coming to power. Sure enough, that first Christmas, a huge star appeared in the sky. The Bible tells us that the wise men followed that star all the way to Bethlehem, where they found the baby Jesus. The wise men brought gifts to the baby Jesus and bowed down and worshiped him because they knew he was the new king.

I want you to pay attention to something very important the wise men did: They followed the star. They looked to the star to guide them to the place they needed to go. None of the wise men said, "Forget that star. I know the right way to find the king. Let's go my way instead." The wise men followed the star.

Like the wise men, we need to be followers. Sometimes we want to be the leader. We want to have our way. We want to be first in line. We want what we want, and we pitch a fit if we don't get our way. But like the wise men, we need to learn how to follow God. We need to put our ways aside and follow God's ways. God is so much bigger and wiser than any of us. He knows how we should live. God wants us to follow his directions for our lives. When we do, he takes care of us, meeting all our needs, loving us all the time, and giving us his peace.

Let's ask God to help us follow him more closely. Dear God, we often want to do things our way. We often throw a fit when we can't be in charge. Help us, Lord, to learn how to follow you. In Jesus's name, amen.

**Field Experience:** We had someone in our church make a great set of wise men costumes. The costumes included plush crowns and fancy boxes representing the gold, frankincense, and myrrh. Since we use these costumes throughout the year for Bible stories involving kings or wealthy people, they are a great investment.

**Other Children's Sermon Possibilities:** I love to teach the children the story of the wise men by giving all the children crowns to wear and leading them around the sanctuary to find the baby Jesus. You can have someone place a manger with a baby doll in it at the front of the sanctuary while you are traveling with the children. Be sure to hang a star close by. Lead the children to kneel at the manger. Ask them what kinds of presents they would have brought to the baby Jesus on that first Christmas.

**Bible Text:** Luke 2:1–20

**Message:** Jesus was born so he could die on the cross for the things we do wrong.

**Preparation:** You will need the sign, the star, the cross, the heart cutout, the stable cutouts, a stool for Mary to sit on, the manger, the step stool, and costumes for Mary, Joseph, the angel, the shepherds, and the wise men. Hang the star on the stable cutout. Place the cross and the heart cutout inside the manger.

**Script:** All this month, we have been learning about the characters in the very first Christmas. We've called it "Christmas Night Live!" (*Turn on the sign.*) We have talked about Mary and Joseph. (*Have Mary and Joseph take their places in the stable.*) Mary and Joseph said "Yes!" when God asked them to be Jesus's parents on earth. Then we learned about the angels. (*Have the angels take their places in the stable.*) They praised God, which means they gave God credit for doing great things on earth. We talked about the shepherds. They hurried; they ran to find the baby Jesus. (*To the shepherds:*) Shepherds, run up here and take your places. Finally, we learned about the wise men who followed the star (*point to the star*) to find the baby Jesus. (*Have the wise men take their places in the stable scene.*)

When Jesus was born, his parents put him in a manger to sleep. (*Point to the manger.*) Does anyone know what a manger is? (*Listen to the responses.*) It is a feeding box for animals. A manger certainly is an unusual bed for a baby. But Jesus was no ordinary baby. Do any of you know why God sent Jesus to earth to be born as a baby? (*Listen to the responses and then pull the cross out of the manger. Hold the cross up for all the children to see.*) Jesus came to earth to die on the cross so we could be forgiven for our sins, for the things we do wrong. Do you know why Jesus died on the cross? (*Pull the heart cutout from the manger and attach it to the front of the cross.*) Because God loves us so much. The first Christmas reminds us of the cross and God's amazing love for each one of us.

Let's pray together. Dear God, your love for us is so huge. Thank you for sending Jesus to earth to be born as a baby. Thank you for the cross. We love you, Lord. Amen.

**Field Experience:** I recommend picking your child volunteers in advance for this last Sunday. Get them into their costumes before the children's sermon begins. They can start off sitting with the rest of the children and then come forward at your direction.

**Take-Home Component:** Put together simple "Christmas Cross Ornament Kits" to pass out to the children after the service. These kits should include: two craft sticks, a red foam heart, a two-inch length of red yarn, and instructions for assembly.

Instructions:
1. Glue the craft sticks together in the shape of a cross.
2. Glue the heart to the front of the cross.
3. Shape the yarn into a loop and glue it to the back of the cross.
4. After the glue has dried, hang the cross ornament on your Christmas tree.

# A Portrait of Jesus

## *Introduction*

This series of children's sermons involves an artist creating a portrait of Jesus right before the children's eyes. It is a great series leading up to Easter. Each week, the artist adds one feature to the portrait of Jesus, such as his hands, his feet, or his mouth. That feature is linked to a story about Jesus's life and becomes the subject of the children's sermon for that week. By the end of the series, the portrait is complete, and the children will have a deeper understanding of Jesus's character.

If you are not an artist yourself, you will need to recruit one to help you with these children's sermons. When we created this series in our church, our artist selected a portrait of Jesus by another artist to copy. We needed a portrait that showed all of Jesus's body to coincide with all the features we were highlighting. Once the artist found the right image, she lightly traced it in pencil on a large canvas. She completed the weekly feature in color as the children watched her. During the week, she filled in the portrait more completely.

You will need an easel for the portrait and a stool for the artist. We had full-color copies of the portrait made to hand out to the children on the last Sunday of the series.

You need plenty of lead time to develop this children's sermon and to recruit an artist. Your artist will need to be available for five Sundays.

In addition, it is important to practice the staging and timing of the children's sermon with the artist in advance. He or she will need to know how much time is available to work and how to be sensitive to the children wanting to see the work unfold.

**Bible Text:** John 11

**Message:** Jesus understands how it feels to be sad.

**Preparation:** During this children's sermon, the artist will draw the eyes of Jesus. He or she will need an easel and a stool (if desired). Be sure to position the artist where the children can see the work. Make sure the artist moves out of the way from time to time so the children can observe the progress.

**Script:** For the next few weeks, we are going to watch something very special. (*Artist's name*) is going to draw a picture of Jesus. Each week (*name*) will add another detail to the picture. Each week we will learn another detail about who Jesus is and what he did when he lived on earth.

Today our artist is drawing Jesus's eyes. We don't know exactly what color his eyes were because the Bible doesn't tell us. But many of the people born in the part of the world where Jesus lived have dark-colored eyes. Our artist is going to give Jesus brown eyes in this picture.

Jesus did many things with his eyes that we do with our eyes. He opened them to see. (*Point to your open eyes.*) He closed them when he went to bed. (*Close your eyes.*) He blinked (*blink your eyes*) and winked (*wink your eye*). Did you know that Jesus even cried?

The Bible (*hold up your Bible open to John 11*) tells the story of a time when Jesus cried. Jesus had three good friends—Lazarus and his sisters, Mary and Martha. He loved them very much. One day, Jesus's friend Lazarus got very sick. The doctors could not make Lazarus well. He got sicker and sicker until he died. Jesus went to Lazarus's house. When he arrived, Mary and Martha were crying; they were sad because their brother had died. The Bible says that when Jesus saw Mary and Martha and the other people crying, he was deeply troubled and saddened. Jesus cried. Jesus understands how it feels when someone we love dies. He knows how much that hurts.

That's one of many great things about Jesus. He understands how we feel. The next time you feel sad about anything, you can talk to Jesus. Tell him how you feel, and you will feel his Spirit comfort you.

This story has a good ending. Jesus went to Lazarus's tomb and called for Lazarus to come out. By the power of Jesus's words, Lazarus came back to life again and walked right out of the tomb. As you can imagine, all that crying stopped pretty quickly! Everyone was amazed at Jesus's power. Even today, Jesus has power over death. If we believe in him, when we die, we will go to live with him in heaven forever. With Jesus, we are guaranteed that our lives will have a good ending too.

Let's pray together. Jesus, you understand how it feels to be sad. You know what it is like to cry. Help us to come to you when we are sad and talk to you about our feelings. We love you so much. Amen.

**Field Experience:** I like to use the time when the children are coming forward for the children's sermon to talk to them individually. My microphone is not on at that point, so it's not an official part of my message. This informal greeting time gives me a chance to say a personal word of encouragement to them so they feel welcomed to "big church."

**Other Children's Sermon Possibilities:** I think it is important to remind children that Jesus was like a regular person. When Jesus was in the wilderness for forty days and nights, he became hungry (see Matt. 4:2). In John 4:6

we read that Jesus was tired from a long journey. When the disciples tried to keep children away from him, Jesus became angry (see Mark 10:14). By describing how Jesus is like us, we make him accessible to children. Create a children's sermon called "Who Is Jesus" that teaches children about Jesus's divine and human characteristics. This is a good way to introduce them to the doctrine of the incarnation.

## A Portrait of Jesus—His Mouth

**Bible Texts:** Matthew 8:5–13, 23–27; Proverbs 15:4

**Message:** Jesus spoke, and amazing things happened.

**Preparation:** You will need the canvas, an easel, the stool, and the artist.

**Script:** Today our artist is drawing Jesus's mouth. Jesus used his mouth to speak, just like we do. But the words that came out of his mouth had God's power. Jesus spoke, and amazing things happened. In the eighth chapter of the book of Matthew, we find two stories about the power of Jesus's words.

One day, Jesus was traveling to a town called Capernaum. A Roman soldier ran up to him and asked him for help. The soldier was very important in the Roman army. The Bible says he was an officer, which meant that he was such a good soldier he had been put in charge of a group of soldiers. The Roman officer said, "Jesus, please help me. My servant is sick. He cannot move, and he is in great pain." Jesus said, "I will come to your house and help your servant." But the Roman officer replied, "I'm not worthy to have you come to my house. I know that you are a powerful man. Just say the words from right where you are, and my servant will be healed!" That's exactly what Jesus did. He said, "Your servant is healed." Isn't that amazing? All Jesus had to do was speak, and a sick person in a house far away was healed. Jesus's words are powerful.

Another time, Jesus was in a boat on a lake with his disciples. A huge storm came up. The wind was blowing hard. Waves were crashing into the boat. The disciples were frightened, but Jesus was sleeping. The disciples woke him up and said, "Jesus, save us! We're going to drown!" Jesus stood up and told the wind and the waves, "Stop it." And the storm stopped. Isn't that amazing? All Jesus had to do was speak, and a terrible storm stopped. Jesus's words are powerful.

Our words are powerful too. We do not have the same kind of power Jesus had when he spoke, but the Bible says our words are powerful enough to help someone or to hurt someone. In Proverbs 15:4 (NLT) we read: "Gentle words bring life and health; a deceitful tongue crushes the spirit." When you tell someone, "I'm glad you're my friend; you did a good job; way to go," your words help the person feel better. But when you say to someone, "I don't like you; I don't want to play with you; you are stupid," your words make the person feel bad.

Let's pray and ask God to help us use our words in ways that help other people, just as Jesus used his powerful words to do amazing things. Dear Jesus, you are so powerful. You speak, and good things happen. Help me, Lord, to speak words that make people feel good. In your name, amen.

**Field Experience:** Maintaining control of the children while you are talking is an important skill that you can hone over time. For example, if a child is talking while you are talking, make eye contact with the child and place your finger to your lips to indicate that you want the child to stop talking. If a child continues to chatter, reach over and gently place your hand on his or her mouth. The idea is to quickly fix disruptive behavior without disrupting the flow of your message.

**Other Children's Sermon Possibilities:** Another way to teach Proverbs 15:4 is to use a knife and a bandage. Tell the children, "There are two ways you can use words. You can use your words like a knife. You can cut people down. You can hurt them by making fun of them. Or, you can use your words like a bandage. You can use words to make people feel better. You can use your words to heal their hurt feelings."

## A Portrait of Jesus—His Feet

**Bible Text**: John 12:1–3

**Message:** Jesus is the only person we should worship.

**Preparation:** You will need the canvas, an easel, the stool, and the artist.

**Script:** Good morning! We are in the process of creating a portrait of Jesus. So far we have watched our artist draw Jesus's eyes. Jesus's eyes remind us of the time Jesus cried when his good friend Lazarus died. We know we can talk to

Jesus when we are feeling sad because he understands how we feel. As our artist drew Jesus's mouth, we talked about the times Jesus spoke words and miracles happened. We know that our words can be powerful too. The things we say can help people feel better. Today our artist is going to draw Jesus's feet. Can you think of any stories in the Bible about Jesus's feet? (*Listen to the responses.*)

In the book of John there is a special story about Jesus and his feet. Jesus was at Lazarus's house—the same Lazarus Jesus raised from the dead. Martha and Mary were there. They were having a dinner party for Jesus. Mary knew that Jesus was the Son of God. She knew that Jesus was like no other person who had ever lived on earth. Mary loved Jesus for who he was and for the many miracles he had performed. She wanted to do something at the dinner party to show Jesus how important he was to her. So Mary took a jar of very expensive perfume, and she gently poured the perfume over Jesus's feet. Then Mary wiped his feet with her hair. The Bible says the whole house was filled with the sweet smell of the perfume.

Now all this may sound a little strange to you. Pouring perfume over someone's feet is not something we do, but when Jesus was alive, it was the custom for servants to wash people's feet when they came inside a house. Mary washed Jesus's feet in the best way she knew how—with expensive perfume. She wanted to show that she loved Jesus more than anyone else. She worshiped Jesus. Jesus was Mary's hero.

Today, there are a lot of people we might think of as heroes. Maybe you have a favorite athlete or a favorite singer or a favorite movie star. You might even have a favorite teacher. It's great to look up to important people in our lives, but the Bible teaches us that there is no person we should love more than Jesus. That's what the story of Jesus's feet reminds us to do—to worship Jesus, just as Mary did.

Let's pray together. Dear Jesus, you are our hero. We love you more than anyone else. Amen.

**Field Experience:** When I led this children's sermon, I asked the children an open-ended question: "Can you think of any stories in the Bible about Jesus's feet?" Open-ended questions can be tricky because you never know how the children will answer. But sometimes it is worth the risk to hear what children are thinking. This time it worked. A second-grade boy raised his hand and said, "There is the story of John baptizing Jesus and John said, 'I am not worthy to tie the sandals on Jesus's feet.'" It was a reference I had not even considered. I was able to affirm him by saying, "That's a great one. I can tell you have been reading your Bible. The one I want to focus on today is . . ."

**Other Children's Sermon Possibilities:** Another story about feet is the story of Jesus washing the disciples' feet. Call a child forward and wash his or her feet as you teach the children about the biblical custom. Give children examples of how they can serve people just as Jesus served his disciples.

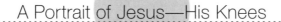

# A Portrait of Jesus—His Knees

**Bible Text:** Luke 22:39–42

**Message:** Jesus teaches us to follow God's way.

**Preparation:** You will need the canvas, an easel, the stool, and the artist.

**Script:** We are studying different stories about Jesus, using this picture of Jesus that our artist is drawing. So far, we have talked about Jesus's eyes and mouth and feet. Today our artist is going to draw Jesus's knees.

Very close to the time Jesus was to die on the cross, he went to a garden with his disciples. When they got to the garden, Jesus left the disciples at one spot and told them to pray. Then he went farther into the garden and got down on his knees to pray. Let's get on our knees. (*Get on your knees with the children.*) Raise your hand if you ever get on your knees when you pray. (*Let the children respond.*) Good. There are a lot of different ways we can pray. We can pray standing up. We can pray sitting down. We can even pray when we're lying in bed. But getting on our knees is one really great way to pray. It's a way of showing with our bodies that we are bowing down before God—that God is in control of our lives.

Jesus got on his knees and prayed these words: "Father, please keep me from this suffering." You see, Jesus knew that he would die on the cross for the things people do wrong, and he knew it would be painful. Jesus was honest with his heavenly Father about how he was feeling. But then Jesus finished his prayer by saying: "God, I will follow your way, not my own way." Say that after me: "God, I will follow your way (*children repeat*), not my own way" (*children repeat*). While Jesus was praying, the Bible says an angel from heaven appeared and strengthened him. Soon after that, the soldiers came to arrest Jesus.

As followers of Jesus, there are things we need to do that we don't always feel like doing. Sometimes we need to obey our parents, but we don't feel like obeying. Sometimes we need to treat someone nicely, but we don't feel like being nice. Sometimes we need to share our toys, our food, or our money, but we don't feel like sharing. Whenever there is something you need to do that you don't feel like doing, I want you to get on your knees. I want you to remember that God is in control of your life. You can be honest with God and tell him how you feel. And then end your prayer by saying, "God, I will follow your way (*direct children to repeat after you*), not my own way" (*children repeat*). When you pray like this, God will strengthen you to do things his way. That's what we can learn from this picture of Jesus's knees (*point to the portrait*).

Pray with me, please. Dear God, it is hard for us to do things we don't feel like doing. But Jesus was willing to do everything for us, even die on the cross. Help us to follow your way. We love you, Lord. Amen.

**Field Experience:** It is important to provide specific examples of how children can apply biblical principles to their daily lives. It is not enough to say, "You need to follow God's way." You must put words to exactly what that looks like for children. The more specific you can be in teaching children how to live out their faith, the better.

**Other Children's Sermon Possibilities:** Create a children's sermon that contrasts Adam and Eve's disobedience in the Garden of Eden with Jesus's prayer of submission in the Garden of Gethsemane. You can make a temporary garden scene using silk trees and plants or cardboard cutouts.

## A Portrait of Jesus—His Hands

**Bible Text:** John 20:24–29

**Message:** Jesus rose from the dead.

**Preparation:** You will need the canvas, an easel, the stool, and the artist.

**Script:** Happy Easter! We have learned a lot about Jesus from this picture our artist has been drawing. We have learned that Jesus cried when his friend Lazarus died. We have learned that the words that came from Jesus's mouth were powerful enough to heal people and stop storms. We have learned that Jesus is the only person we should worship—just like Mary worshiped Jesus by pouring perfume over his feet. We have also learned that Jesus got down on his knees and prayed for strength to follow God's way before he was arrested and taken to the cross to die.

Today our artist is completing our portrait by drawing Jesus's hands. Jesus did some amazing things while he was on earth. He changed water into wine. He healed people and raised people from the dead. He even walked on water. But one of the most amazing things Jesus did was to die on the cross and come back to life again. Some people have a hard time believing that this is really true. In fact, Thomas, one of Jesus's disciples, had a hard time believing that Jesus was alive. Listen to what the Bible says: "One of the disciples, Thomas . . . , was not with the others when Jesus came. They told him, 'We have seen the Lord!' But [Thomas] replied, 'I won't believe it unless I see the nail wounds in his hands, put my fingers into them'" (John 20:24–25 NLT).

You remember that Jesus was nailed to the cross through his hands and feet. Thomas was saying, "If Jesus has really come back to life, I need to see it for myself. I need to see the marks the nails left in his hands to know that this is really true."

The Bible tells us what happened next: "Eight days later the disciples were together again, and this time Thomas was with them. The doors were locked; but suddenly, as before, Jesus was standing among them. He said, 'Peace be with you.' Then he said to Thomas, 'Put your finger here and see my hands. . . . Don't be faithless any longer. Believe!'" (John 20:26–27 NLT).

Jesus died on the cross and came back to life again. When we think of Jesus's hands, that's what we need to remember. Sometimes we may feel a little bit like the disciple Thomas. Sometimes we may worry or wonder if the things we read in the Bible are true. Sometimes we may have questions about God and Jesus that no grown-up is able to answer for us. That is okay. There are many things that we will not completely understand until we get to heaven. But while we are here on earth, Jesus wants us to do the same thing he wanted Thomas to do: believe!

Let's pray together. Dear Jesus, you are amazing. Only you can die on a cross and come back to life again. Only you can give us forgiveness for the things we do wrong and life forever in heaven. We believe in you! Amen.

**Field Experience:** You may wonder how much detail you should provide about Jesus's death on the cross. It is a gruesome thing for adults to think about, much less children. I believe it is important to tell children the facts about Jesus's death but not to dwell on them. You do not need to gloss over the harsh realities of the gospel story, but you do need to expose children to manageable pieces of information.

**Other Children's Sermon Possibilities:** Hebrews 11:1 is a great verse to teach children. "Faith is being sure of what we hope for and certain of what we do not see." We cannot see air, but we know it is there. We cannot see love, but we know what it feels like. We cannot see God, but we believe in him. Teach children that faith means believing now what we will see later.

# Notes

## Chapter 1 Children in "Big Church"

1. George Barna, *Transforming Children into Spiritual Champions* (Ventura, CA: Regal, 2003), 45.

2. Ivy Beckwith, *Postmodern Children's Ministry: Ministry to Children in the 21st Century* (El Cajon, CA: Youth Specialties, 2004), 148–49.

3. Ibid., 142.

4. J. Otis and Gail Ledbetter and Jim and Janet Weidmann, *Spiritual Milestones: A Guide to Celebrating Your Child's Spiritual Passages* (Colorado Springs: Cook, 2001), 12.

5. Ibid.

6. Ibid.

## Chapter 2 Buy One, Get One Free

1. Brant D. Baker, *Let the Children Come: A New Approach to Children's Sermons* (Minneapolis: Augsburg, 1991), 8.

2. Ibid., 20–21.

3. Beckwith, *Postmodern Children's Ministry*, 52–53.

## Chapter 4 Preparing for Children's Sermon Success

1. Baker, *Let the Children Come*, 16.

## Chapter 6 Concept-Driven Children's Sermons

1. Baker, *Let the Children Come*, 12.

**Beth Edington Hewitt**, a mother of two, has an M.A. in Christian education and specializes in children's ministry. She has served churches in Selma, Alabama, and Orlando, Florida, where she worked for six years leading a children's program of three hundred children.

252.53
H6112

112003

LINCOLN CHRISTIAN COLLEGE AND SEMINARY

3 4711 00176 3822